A
White Guy
Confronting
Racism

An Invitation to
Reflect and Act

JARED KAROL

Foreword by Madison Butler

1st Edition, 1st printing 2021

Editor: Richard Tardiff

Author Photo: Gani Piñero

Cover Concept Design and Interior Design:

Steve Walters, Oxygen Publishing Inc

Independently Published by
Oxygen Publishing Inc.
Montreal, QC, Canada
www.oxygenpublishing.com

ISBN: 978-1-990093-16-6

Imprint: Independently published

Dedication

For Erica, Juliet, and Max.

And for Dad.

I think you'd be proud of who I've become.

What's said...

Jared Karol writes "the personal is universal," and walks the talk in this book, transparently sharing his own journey, from self-described bomb-thrower for change to a more nuanced—and I'd say more effective—voice and approach. As one of the few books written by a straight cisgender White man on this topic, his candid examination of his own awakening, outrage, and accountability to himself and others hold many helpful insights for all of us—in our attempts to do more, and to step into the ownership of a more equitable, shared future.

– **Jennifer Brown**, CEO of Jennifer Brown Consulting; Author, *Inclusion* (2017) and *How to Be an Inclusive Leader* (2019); Podcast Host, *The Will to Change*

Jared Karol models what it means to show up every day for racial justice. *A White Guy Confronting Racism* challenges White people—and all of us—to show up and do the work. Written with clear conviction and courageous vulnerability, this book will serve as a guide for anyone who is still figuring out who they want to be in the fight for equity and racial justice.

– **Dr. Nika White**, President and CEO of Nika White Consulting; Author, *The Intentional Inclusionist and Next Level Inclusionist: Transform Your Work and Yourself for Diversity, Equity, and Inclusion Success*

When I started seeing Jared's posts on LinkedIn, I knew he was on to something. His commitment, his eloquence, his ability to stand in solidarity with melanated communities and in direct opposition to the standardization of white-bodied communities had me reading every single one of his posts that came into my feed. I hope this book enlightens you, excites you, invites you to show up more empathetically and with greater understanding for multiple sets of rules at play in our current infrastructures. I hope this book propels you to take a stance, to connect more deeply to yourself, and to build a global community more saliently than ever before. Jared's words did that for me.

– **Rajkumari Neogy**, Executive Coach; Epigenetics and Neurobiology; Founder of iBelong

Jared Karol isn't just another White guy who needs to see his name on the cover of a book. He's an extremely open-minded White guy who cares deeply about people and the future of humanity. In *A White Guy Confronting Racism*, Jared strips away all pretense and delivers a deeply personal account of his journey to becoming antiracist, while providing guidance to those of us who may be compelled to take similar action. Along the way, he confronts his own White privilege and ignorance head-on with short vignettes that are embarrassing in retrospect, often funny, and always full of powerful, teachable moments. The White guy narrative was easy for this White guy to identify with and I learned a lot about why I should care, how I can help combat racism with compassion, and how truth is the antiracist's best ally. We are the ones who are fortunate to have Jared's name on the cover of this meaningful book.

– **Evan Birkhead**, Tech Marketing Professional & Activist; Another White Guy Confronting Racism

When I have seen racism or inequality, I have often kept to myself—either too scared or uncomfortable to speak out. As an upper middle class White male, I worried about saying the wrong thing and inadvertently offending people. I preferred to listen and attempt to understand. That felt safer than actually doing something. Jared has helped me to realize that being antiracist takes courage and action.

– **Mike Walsh**, Technology Sales Executive

~

Jared fearlessly interrogates his own privilege and caringly invites others to interrogate theirs. White supremacy requires courage and wisdom from White people to do the work of dismantling it. Jared is a strong and skillful leader in that work, and his book is a superb guide for others to work at the emotional, spiritual, and practical levels needed.

– **Mansi Goel**, Executive Coach; Leadership Development Facilitator at The Graduate School of Business at Stanford; previously Google's Global Head of Product Policy

~

Amidst America's great reckoning with racism, Jared and I began to build a friendship often circling back to two of our personal values: demonstrating empathy and beginning conversations. As I've read *A White Guy Confronting Racism*, it's hard for me to imagine two better ways to characterize the book. Both personal and universal in its approach, Jared invites us all into conversation—regardless of our racial background—to better envision how we can embrace many lived experiences, because we need them all.

– **Jeremy Evans-Smith**, DEI Talent Leader; Founder of Ascending

In a time when the world is more divided and fragile than ever, Jared's book invites us to have a human conversation of reflection, connectivity, and accountability. Even though Jared and I come from vastly different worlds, each chapter mirrors many of my own experiences. As a Black Queer woman with a family from Birmingham, AL, I was taught not to trust White people for my own survival. My journey in building a relationship with Jared (as you will do in the pages of this book) has allowed me the space to collaborate with him to break the chains of our shared prison that is systemic racism. And yes, I encouraged him to write this book specifically because he is a White man. We need more White men like him to help deconstruct the racist systems that impede our collective prosperity. Jared, thank you for doing the work and sharing your story. Thank you, reader, for joining us on this journey. Welcome to the conversation.

– **Dominique Hollins,** Founder & Connector-in-Chief, WĒ360, LLC

Jared's ability to create a safe space to discuss systemic racism for people of all backgrounds is a gift. His life-long dedication to equity and bridging cultural gaps shows in everything he does. This book is a must-read for anyone who wants to be a part of the social justice movement in creating lasting change.

– **Amanda Townsend**, CEO, BoldChange

White people, we need to change. NOW! I hope you see yourself in Jared's story and that he inspires you to take action.

– **Karen Fleshman**, Founder of Racy Conversations

Table of Contents

Foreword

From the first page to the final vignette of *A White Guy Confronting Racism*, Jared Karol disrupts the status quo of whiteness by unapologetically recognizing Black humanity. With a rare and refreshing combination of vulnerability, humility, and conviction, he challenges other White people to do the same. This book shares hard truths about racism that White people need to hear, without depending on dogma or dipping into self-righteousness. Knowing that White people often hear the message more clearly from another White person, Jared has stepped up to deliver it.

One thread that is clear throughout this book is that it has never been enough to be "not racist." We must be fiercely antiracist in all facets of our existence. Too often we skirt around the difficult conversations and the introspection that makes us uncomfortable. Looking inside ourselves to examine the ugly parts is painful. Acknowledging our role in another's trauma can be heartbreaking. I know, because I have been there. We all cause harm. What matters is what we do with that knowledge and with our power.

Antiracism work was never meant to be easy. If you are having conversations that only feel like hugs, you are having the wrong conversations. Oppression is not warm, fuzzy, and pretty—it is ugly. Looking in the mirror to understand the harm you have caused in your lifetime, and acknowledging the ways you have upheld White supremacy, is painful—and necessary. But looking in the mirror is only part of the work; it is the catalyst that shapes the lens through which you view the world.

Jared invites you to self-reflect, with the clear expectation that you will hold yourself accountable and transform reflection into action. Antiracism work is about how we impact the people and communities around us.

As a Black woman, I do not have a choice but to show up in my skin every day. I cannot step away from the risk of being Black. Black women spend every moment looking over our shoulders, holding our breath. There is privilege in looking away from the plight of those who are different, but I encourage you to look White supremacy in the eye and promise to do better. White people, I encourage you to step into a place where you can get comfortable being uncomfortable. Remember that while you only have to be uncomfortable, Black Americans are living in fear.

Take a moment to think about the last time you felt fear, real fear, the kind that claws at the bottom of your stomach. The kind of fear that leaves the back of your knees moist, and the back of your throat dry. This is the fear that Black America feels every day.

When we go to the grocery store.

When we are walking home.

When we are watching the police lights dance in our rearview mirror.

We feel fear when we look into our babies' eyes because we know we cannot protect them.

We live in fight-or-flight mode because of White supremacy.

White supremacy harms you too, it is just quieter. White supremacy is the monster under all of our beds. It has been preying on Black and brown people for centuries, and we deserve not to be the only ones fighting and looking it in the eye. This monster may not scare you, but it sneaks in unnoticed, lingering in the corners of your home, infiltrating your conversations, influencing your habits.

There is privilege in being able to exist safely, to never have to look over your shoulder while putting the key into your own door. We all must be willing to use that privilege and power to create a better world for the next generations. If Black families have to teach our children how to survive in a world that only intends to harm them, White people can commit to teaching their children not to kill ours.

A White Guy Confronting Racism challenges us to reach in and pull out the ugliness that society has planted inside of us. Society's idea of "the right way to exist" has been embedded into our brains for as long as we have been alive. We are taught that the world exists in binary terms. People are White or Black. People are straight or gay. People are tall or short. And the list goes on. But here's the secret: nothing is binary. We must be willing to step outside our comfort zone and into the grey area. We must be committed to unlearning the societal norms that have been forced upon us.

The ugliness of White supremacy is often too daunting for White people to truly unpack within themselves, so they limit their commitment to tolerating, understanding, and empathizing with people who are marginalized and oppressed. But that will never be enough.

Tolerance is not enough.

Acceptance is not enough.

Hashtags are not enough.

Warm and fuzzy presentations on diversity are not enough.

Joining a diversity book club is not enough.

Signing a diversity pledge is not enough.

Kindness is not enough.

Niceties will not dismantle White supremacy or patriarchal standards. We need more than empathy. We need co-conspirators who are willing to fight alongside us. We need White people to take the burden of oppression off our shoulders, to do the emotional labor, to be willing to defend our lives in a world that was never meant to love us.

We need you. You must be actively and unapologetically anti-racist. There is always more than one side to history. You get to choose the right one.

This book will call you out for perpetuating White supremacy and systemic racism, and importantly, it will call you into conversations about racism.

And that's all part of the work. Jared is asking you to do the work. I am asking you to do the work.

Do the work.

Madison Butler

VP of People + Impact at GRAV

Founder of Blue Haired Unicorn

Introduction

I Wasn't Broke, But I Was Badly Bent

*"I don't believe your antiracist work is complete
or valid or useful if you haven't engaged
with Black humanity."* – Tarana Burke

The Deschutes Brewery in Bend, Oregon, was packed with customers that Friday afternoon in mid-September 2015. My friend and I were finishing our third round of beers and waiting for the check. We invited two guys to join us to avoid the wait and take our table when we were done. They were in town from eastern Oregon to do some fishing and drink some beers. We were up from California for a long weekend to float down the Deschutes River and explore the town.

"Where in California?" one guy asked.

"Both from San Diego," I said. "But now I live in Oakland."

"Oakland?" he said. Eyebrows raised. Emerging smirk. "There are tons of Black people in Oakland, aren't there?"

He emphasized "tons," elongating it into two syllables. I sensed a condemnation of my moral character, a provocative mixture of mockery, sympathy, and bewilderment around why I, a White guy like him, would choose to live in Oakland and be weighted down beneath the many tons of Black people.

"There are a lot of Black people in Oakland," I said. "Maybe about a hundred thousand."

Not picking up my conciliatory tone, he shook his head. "I was in the Bay Area once."

Looking at me for confirmation that I understood that what he was about to say was important, he said, "I got on the BART train in Pleasanton. And there were all White people." Pause. Then, "As I made it into Oakland, there were aaallll Black people." Another pause. Spreading his arms wide, indicating the totality of blackness on this long-ago BART ride in deep, deep, black, black Oakland, he looked around the white, white Bend brewery, as if the White beer drinkers had morphed into a beer drinking Black mob. Another shake of the head, to emphasize the derision, or clear the memories.

"As I went into San Francisco?" he said with an uplift, an invitation for me to show how rapt I was by his story. Pause. "There were all Chinese people." Pause. A dramatic sip of beer. The silence of our little group was broken only by the cheer and camaraderie of White beer drinkers on a Friday afternoon, in an idyllic mountain town in central Oregon.

I was waiting to hear more of the story, some clever insight, some unexpected turn of events, something funny or awful or unusual or—something! But after a few moments of awkward silence, it became clear his last pause was the final pause. His story was simply a racial demographic breakdown of one man's BART ride, with the unspoken but clear implication that White Pleasanton was safe and desirable, that Black Oakland was dangerous and undesirable, and that San Francisco would have been okay if it weren't for all those Chinese people.

He was stating the obvious. Things that anyone who was paying attention would notice and infer. And because our little group was all White, anything else said would surely be redundant, a waste of breath, and unnecessary.

It was clear that our shared whiteness elevated us to a special superior shared understanding and shared appreciation and shared recognition of our shared condescending opinion about Black people, which also meant we could talk openly and candidly and dismissively about Black people. No damage had been done to any Black people by White people talking this way about Black people. To doubt or question or challenge this was not how the play was written. And it was not okay to go off script.

By the time I had thought of how to respond, we paid our check, finished our beers, and said our goodbyes. We may have even shaken hands.

On the walk back to our place I said to my friend, "That was an interesting conversation." I urgently wanted to talk with someone about what we had just experienced, to break it down, to provide commentary and analysis, to explore deeper meanings and ramifications and contexts. I knew all too well that my present company would not give me that opportunity, and would not have the interest or patience to discuss.

"What do you mean?" he asked. "I thought those guys were pretty cool."

"What do I mean?" I said, trying to find the right balance of how can you not know what I mean; and I know too well that you don't know what I mean? "What I mean is, who starts a conversation with total strangers with racist observations about a guy's hometown?"

"Dude!" he said. "Sometimes I wonder if you live in Oakland so that you can talk about race and Black people all the time."

And with a bang, the conversation slammed shut. We walked the rest of the way in silence. The devolution of the guys' weekend had begun within hours of our arrival. If only it were the first incident, I would have been surprised, angry, hurt, combative. But no, the pattern was similar to so many other experiences we shared around race and racism over the past fifteen years. It had become something to endure, to try to overcome, something to constantly decide if and how to address the widening chasm of our friendship, which had slowly opened up a distance that was increasingly unnavigable.

After the trip, as we drove to the airport along the 880 freeway in Oakland, a giant Black Lives Matter banner appeared draped across a building's brick wall.

"What do you think of Black Lives Matter?" he asked.

I chose my words carefully. "The way I see it, Black Lives Matter is about Black humanity. Black Lives Matter exists out of necessity because Black people have been unfairly harassed and unjustly killed by the police."

"Hmmpf," he said, not unfriendly. Perhaps he, too, was acutely aware of the chasm. We drove in silence for a few seconds. Then he said, "I just think that all lives matter."

~

Meanwhile, my job was sucking the life out of me. I had left my role as a middle school social justice teacher in 2011 after twelve years in the classroom, for a job as an editorial assistant at a startup in the personalized shopping space—about as sexy and prestigious as it sounds. Initially, I enjoyed my new career. But the novelty of publishing 2-for-1 coupons on women's socks at Macy's and benchmarking what qualified as a "great deal" in the auto parts industry had worn off. The work was dull, paid poorly, had no room for growth, and put me in a bad mood every day. I was stuck.

My neighbor suggested I explore working with a coach he had used a few years back. Having never been to a coach and having no idea how it worked, I asked about her. "She's kind of a career coach," he said, "and kind of a life coach, and kind of a wisdom coach. She isn't cheap, but she's good."

An expensive wisdom coach? I prevented a snide comment from being said out loud. And then I thought, "I'm desperate for some wisdom right about now."

After a few calls to understand how she worked, I plopped down more money on her than on anything I had ever purchased that wasn't a house or a car. I was nervous and excited, not knowing what she could do for me or what wisdom I could hope to gain about myself, my career, and my life. It turned out to be the wisest investment I ever made. Over two intense back-to-back seven-hour sessions and a few follow-up meetings, she realigned me with my purpose, and set the direction for how I would make a real impact on real people in the real world.

She said, "You're a social justice guy. You gotta get back to that work. We don't know at this moment what that work is going to be or what it's going to look like, but you gotta get back to that work. You are inherently curious and compassionate. You're always seeking profound and genuine connections with people. You have an innate ability to see the world through unique and disparate perspectives. You are inspired by acts of social justice. You orchestrate and build inclusive communities by acknowledging and celebrating differences. You are always empowering individuals and communities to provide appropriate resources that make room for fulfillment and hope. You celebrate every person's right to thrive. You believe that positive social impact is essential to a fulfilling life. You always—always—see the humanity in people."

Those were her exact words. They became my exact words. We typed them into a document that I saved on my computer. But we didn't arrive at this clarity automagically. No, it had to come pouring out of me. I had to share my personal and professional life story with her, and because I didn't know where else to start, I started at the beginning.

I told her about a seventeen-year-old girl in Urbana, Illinois, who needed to get the hell out of her house because of her alcoholic and racist father, and how she met a twenty-one-year-old drifter back from helping Castro with the sugar harvests in Cuba, and how as soon as that girl turned eighteen they eloped and moved to New Mexico. One year later, they had a baby boy, and they named him Jared Isaac, biblical names, even though neither was religious in the slightest.

And I told her that if we lived in an equitable world, none of that would have happened, and I would never have been born because that man, my father, Arnold Stanley Karol, was gay, but he couldn't tell anyone because it wasn't okay or safe or legal to be gay in the early 1970s in the Midwest or the Southwest or most anywhere in the United States. You did what you were expected to do, and you married a woman, had a kid, and led a "normal" life. You suppressed your identity.

I told her how my father had tried to commit suicide twice before he was eighteen because of the shame and confusion and stigma and isolation, and how I felt those same feelings when I turned fourteen, and my dad told me he was gay, long after he had earned an English degree from the University of New Mexico, and after we had all moved to San Diego, and after my parents had split up because my dad found the courage to tell the world he was gay, and after he had moved up to LA and then to San Francisco to live how he wanted to live and be who he wanted to be.

And I told her how I cried when my dad told me he was gay. I was a fourteen-year-old homophobic boy in the late eighties, embarrassed, unprepared to have a gay dad. I told her how I didn't know any gay people until then, and how I wasn't going to tell anyone about my dad. I kept my secret, constantly worried that somehow someone would find out and tease me and mock me and ridicule me and spread rumors about me, and expose the truth, and how this would wreck my bright, shiny non-gay-dad-having image I presented to the world.

I told her how when I was twenty years old I found the nerve to tell my friend Amy that I had a gay dad, and how she looked at me with an empathetic smile and casually said, "big fucking deal." I felt this huge weight being lifted, and I realized I didn't have to keep living this bullshit, narrow, and false narrative of who I thought I was, and who I could and would and should become. Amy's nonchalant and compassionate and simple and nonjudgmental acceptance of my reality was the permission I needed to grow into the authentic, dynamic, and compelling version of myself. None of that happened right away, but even if on that night when I told Amy my dad was gay I could not have articulated to myself or told anyone else how it was going to happen, I knew it was going to happen and I was determined to make it happen.

And I told my coach how this transformation opened up a new world of possibilities, how it allowed my dad and me to have a much stronger relationship, and how it provided a springboard for me to jump into the ocean of life and explore and immerse and experience with the firm belief that even if the waves got big and the currents got strong and the winds blew with gale force that I would not drown, that I would persevere, that I would survive, thrive, and make an impact, affect the lives of other people positively, share my voice, my story, my truth.

I told her how seven years later that transformation from who I was to who I would become was only just out of its embryonic stages when my dad died of AIDS. I cried in front of my coach in that little office space as I told her how I cried tears of heartache and loss and sorrow and deep, deep sadness when my dad died. I told her how I was too far on my journey now to go back to who I was, and how I was inspired and empowered and called upon by my dad to no longer be that guy who didn't care and didn't know and didn't understand and didn't appreciate the lived experiences of people not like me. I told her, crying, how through being with my dad and embracing his story and his reality and his perspective on life, I was able to infinitely and perpetually expand my story and my reality, and my perspective on life.

I told her that around that time when my dad passed away, one of my biggest emerging understandings and realizations was my immense and chronic failure to see every person as human, how by choosing to not see the humanity in other people because they were different than me, or because I perceived them to be different than me, how I missed out on countless opportunities to experience the vast dynamism of the human condition, to learn from and with other people, to love and respect other people, to uplift and amplify the voices of other people, to create opportunity and drive impact and affect change for other people.

And I told her how seamless it was to understand that the marginalization and oppression and discrimination that my dad and the LGBTQ community faced was similar to the marginalization and oppression and discrimination that all underrepresented groups face, because of their race or their religion or their class or their language or their income level or their accent or their ability or their gender identity or their immigration status. I told her how through what my dad taught me, whether formally or whether through osmosis, I realized that my actions and inactions and who I chose to hang out with and what I chose to read and watch and listen to, and whose voices I chose to amplify and whose voices I chose not to listen to or to hear or to mention, that I was contributing to the continued marginalization and oppression and discrimination that so many individuals and groups of people unfairly, inequitably, inhumanely were forced to deal with daily. I decided that I no longer wanted to be that guy, that I no longer would be that guy, that I no longer was that guy, and that I was going to accelerate my journey and become an unapologetic champion for the underdog, for what's right, for what's good, for what's equitable and just—for humanity.

I told her how I got into teaching because I wanted—desperately needed—to teach kids what I wasn't taught when I was a kid, to contribute to the undoing, the unlearning, the dismantling of frameworks and ideologies and systems and narratives that were negative or damaging or false. I told her how I finally found a school where I could do all this without pushback and questioning and interference and indifference from parents and fellow teachers and administrations, a school that unabashedly was founded on social justice principles, expected its teachers to teach through a social justice lens, and allowed us to teach with autonomy and creativity and authenticity, a school where we could shape young people's minds in a positive, worldly, expansive way, so that they could go forth into the world in a positive, worldly, expansive way, and make that world better compared to my generation and other generations before me.

I told her how much purpose, fulfillment, and agency I felt learning and teaching about social justice principles like power, privilege, inclusion, belonging, impact, equity, and racial justice. It was a dream, too good to be true, to do what I did for a living, making a difference in the lives of so many people. But when my twins were born the demands of teaching and raising two young people was too much to handle, even with the summers off, and I needed a change. I decided I wanted to be a writer, even though I didn't know what I meant by that. I told her how I landed the job at the personalized shopping startup as an editorial assistant, that it was okay for a couple years, but then Macy's and Auto Zone and Home Depot and all their storewide sales, deals of the day, BOGO offers, and up to 60% off coupons started to be the bane of my existence. Every day I was feeling angry, bored, and depressed. I had no purpose or direction. I didn't know what to do or where to go.

And I told her about my recent trip to Bend with my friend, how his views on race were more aligned with those guys we met at the brewery than with mine. I was fine with people having different opinions on things but not being friends with people who were racist. I told her how the trip was another example in a string of examples I could not accept or tolerate—but kept on accepting and tolerating. I told her the trip devolved within hours because of our inability to understand each other, to listen to each other, how it was obvious over the years that we had different and irreconcilable views of the world. I didn't know what to do. It had entered my mind to end the friendship, but that seemed like an impossibility because we had been friends for more than thirty years, and we had many wonderful memories, and his family essentially had raised me from fifth through eighth grade. It was worth holding on to the friendship. There were positive things about the relationship. I tried to think about them, and started to list them, but they seemed so flat and unimportant and irrelevant in comparison to what was bringing us down. I told her how this friendship, and the arguments around race and racism and the inability to engage in civil discussions to explore the deeper implications of our views, not only for the sake of our relationship but for the livelihood of the world, was a major contributing factor to my disillusionment and my professional, personal, emotional, spiritual, and existential crises.

And I told her that all this was how I found my way to her. And that was why I was there with her. And that I hoped she could help me. Please help me?

She listened and asked questions and provided insights and exercises for me to explore. She challenged me to be brave and authentic and true to who I was and my beliefs. In her infinite wisdom, she pushed me to seek and embrace my infinite wisdom, to rediscover my purpose, to realign myself with my principles. She pushed me to be open to the possibilities of what might come to me if I was only vulnerable enough to be open to the possibilities of what might come to me, while reminding me to be uncompromising in my commitment to my values, standards, and ethics.

That was six years ago. It was the platform for who I am today. Everything I discovered and rediscovered about myself back then about social justice and curiosity and compassion and connection and celebrating difference, about empowering people and communities to thrive and always seeing the humanity in people—it's all true today. Even stronger. I still see the humanity in people. I refuse to not see the humanity in people. And I wrote this book as a challenge for you to do the same.

How This Book Came to Exist

He said, "So if you're supposed to be this social justice guy, this White guy who gets it, a writer, a thought leader, a change agent, then how come I don't see you writing anything on LinkedIn?"

I was about to say "I don't know" until I remembered his rule that I could not answer any of his questions with "I don't know." Instead, we sat there at the table in a cafe, looking at each other in silence. His steady stare was a clear challenge for me to step up, to hold myself accountable, to emerge and evolve into the true trailblazer that we had just positioned me as on my resume.

"Do you have something to say?"

"Yes."

"Then say something. Open up your laptop right now and write a post. I'll wait."

He lifted the giant coffee mug to his lips, holding my eyes with his, just above the rim, the steam rising and intermingling with the barely perceptible smirk on his face.

I was ready for the challenge. He had already done so much for me. Six weeks earlier, after an eighteen-month contract with a tech company had ended, I decided I wanted the security and stability of a full-time job instead of hustling for consulting and contract gigs.

I hadn't updated my resume since I left teaching in 2011. It was weak, outdated, and would not land me even an interview, let alone a job.

In three sessions, we worked together to shape a kick-ass resume and build a long-term career strategy, focusing on who I was, what I stood for, and why I was determined to impact the world. This coach doled out much wisdom, helping me make the subtle and vital adjustments that realigned me with my purpose, giving me a much-needed kick in the ass, and challenging me to stop being selfish by not bringing all I had to offer to the world.

I opened up my laptop, went to LinkedIn, wrote something in five minutes, and hit "post." The date was December 18, 2019. He opened up his laptop, left a comment to bring visibility to his couple hundred thousand followers, and said, "I want you to write a post every day until you get a job."

Done. Challenge accepted.

I had plenty to say, and plenty of ability and courage and confidence to say it. I drew on twenty years of writing to re-establish my style, my voice, my point of view. Like you, there was no way in December 2019 I could have predicted what would happen in 2020. I could never have predicted that a global health pandemic would leave us vulnerable, disconnected, and worried for our loved ones and our jobs and futures. I could never have predicted that the pandemic would lead to so many cruel acts of anti-Asian racism. I could never have predicted that a young Black EMT in Louisville, KY named Breonna Taylor would be gunned down in her apartment as she slept, or that a young Black man named Ahmaud Arbery would be murdered with a shotgun as he went for a jog in Georgia, or that a middle-aged White executive named Amy Cooper would weaponize her White privilege and falsely claim in a 911 call that a Black man named Christian Cooper was attacking her in Central Park, or that a police officer in Minneapolis would brutally and tragically murder a Black man named George Floyd who was born only a few months after me, for using a counterfeit twenty-dollar bill. I could not have predicted that the Black community and other communities of color and an increasing number of White people would respond with sustained conviction and power and focus and purpose. I could not have predicted the specific and horrific events enacted by White Supremacists, and how they would continue to exacerbate the political divisiveness that would ultimately lead to an attempted coup at the Capitol building in Washington D.C.

While I could never have predicted any of these events ahead of time, I sure as hell could believe they were happening. I sure as hell could recognize patterns of racist behavior. I sure as hell could see how the systems and institutions operated to uphold White supremacy. I sure as hell could make connections between the past and the present and the possible future. And I sure as hell could write about it.

And so I did.

From December 2019 through January 2021, I wrote nearly three hundred LinkedIn posts about what I was observing and feeling and wanting to change and trying to change. I wrote about racism and empathy and cultural fluency and belonging and mindfulness and leadership and workplace culture and storytelling and vulnerability and much more. I didn't plan any of my posts, other than occasionally keeping some notes in a small notebook I carried around in my pocket. I wrote what was on my mind the day it was on my mind. I typed straight into the LinkedIn "create a post" box, capped by the 1300-character limit. I did no more than minor grammatical editing once they went live. I wrote what I felt was timely and relevant and urgent—and evergreen at the same time. I wrote with a clear and consistent voice that was often inviting, at times challenging, at times philosophical, at times satirical, angry, reflective, and vulnerable. People said: write a book. So, I decided I would write a book. I collected all the posts, kept the best ones, divided them into ten sections, put them in an order that made sense, did some editing, wrote an introduction to each section, and wrote the introduction you're reading now. And here you go—the book you have in your hands.

I never did get that full-time job. But I did get opportunities to facilitate uncomfortable conversations about racism, and opportunities to work one-on-one with leaders on building their antiracist journey, and opportunities to speak and present and share my stories and perspectives and insights about race and racism. Each one of these opportunities has been meaningful and rewarding and important and has contributed in some small way towards the antiracist world that I want to see.

And I did write a book. And the fact that you're reading this book, and presumably will be positively influenced to continue on your antiracist journey, is aligned with my longer-term vision of creating a positive impact in the world.

I'm Not Normal, I'm White

In *The Development of White Identity*, a chapter in Beverly Tatum's book *Why Are All the Black Kids Sitting Together in the Cafeteria?*, she relates how at the beginning of the classes and workshops she leads, she asks participants, "What is your class and ethnic background?" People of color have no problem answering this question. White people, however, don't know how to answer the second part. In her class, one young White woman easily identified as middle class but couldn't find a way to describe herself ethnically. So she landed on, "I'm just normal."

She was—just normal.

When I read Dr. Tatum's book, and especially that chapter, back in 2005, I read that section over and over. She was completely unaware that by declaring herself to be just normal, she was implying that anybody who was not White must be what— abnormal? This concept resonated with me deeply, not because I could make fun of her and other White people, not because I could point the finger at her and other White people, not because I could shake my head at the ignorance of her and other White people. No. What I found profound was how much of me was like that young woman in that class. That for so much of my life, I too saw myself as "just normal." I, too, had no racial or ethnic identity because I had never bothered to explore my racial or ethnic identity. In fact, like that young woman, it had never occurred to me to do so. It wasn't even a blip on my radar screen. With few exceptions, my entire upbringing and social circles and references and world view were White. It, and I, was "just normal."

Now, more than fifteen years later, I can more fully understand and can more clearly recognize and can more deeply appreciate that the majority of White people see themselves as "just normal." Just as that White woman in Dr. Tatum's class did, and just as I did for decades. And because of that clarity, I continue to see how and why it's so problematic. How what may appear on the surface to be innocuous, innocent, and harmless ignorance is anything but. How and why "just normal" perpetuates the status quo, how and why "just normal" perpetuates inequity, how and why "just normal" perpetuates discrimination, how and why "just normal" perpetuates White supremacy, how and why "just normal" perpetuates racism. And how and why White people need to play a crucial role in the fight against racism.

We need to do more than confront racism when we see it in our colleagues, friends, and family, when we see it in our politicians and celebrities, when we see it in our systems and laws and policies and institutions. We need to confront racism when we see it in ourselves. And to see it in ourselves, we need to do the ongoing deep reflection around who we've been, who we are, and who we want to become, so we can take action to end racism. We need to evolve our worldview fundamentally so that "just normal" is no longer a lazy euphemism for "White people." So that "just normal," if it exists, becomes a way to describe the unconditional appreciation and embracing of humanity, whatever our racial background. If each one of us cannot commit to doing this inner work, nothing will change. And whiteness and all that comes with it will continue to be "just normal."

Why You're Reading This Book

*"It's a privilege to not have had to do the work in
your life. You seeking this book out is a step
toward doing this work."* – Rachel Kjack

Perhaps you're a White person who is finally ready and willing
to see the unconditional humanity of Black people. Even though
you know that George Floyd was not the first Black person in
history to be murdered by the police, was not the first Black
person in 2020 to be murdered by the police, maybe something
changed in you when you saw that officer kneeling on George
Floyd's neck for nine minutes, with a casual, smug abuse of power
and unwarranted use of force. An officer, a human being—like
you, like me, like George Floyd—who showed no mercy, who
was deaf to cries for help, who was not willing to entertain the
idea that what he was doing was morally and legally wrong and
unjust, but who was willing to be indifferent and apathetic to the
life of another human being, who was willing to murder.

And maybe as you initially got wind of this blatant, inhumane
murder, and started to read the news reports, and viewed the
video of the killing, and listened to and watched and read the
endless commentary, and observed the outrage and despair and
uprising of Black people who were sick and tired of being treated
like second class citizens and worse for the last four hundred plus
years, perhaps you started to more fully recognize your humanity
too. Perhaps, amid the uncertainty and angst brought about by a
global health pandemic, you recognized your own vulnerability,
desire for connection, and need for safety, love, and belonging.
Perhaps you have begun to realize that you have not been paying
close enough attention to the daily challenges that Black people
and other people of color face.

And perhaps you decided you wanted to do something about
that. Maybe you decided to consciously commit to changing who

you are and how you show up in the world. Maybe you decided to consciously commit to evolving your consciousness, and to taking the empathy and compassion and vulnerability that had previously been reserved only for select people and only in select situations and only for select reasons—maybe you decided that you wanted to be empathetic and compassionate and vulnerable with all people in all situations and for all reasons. And maybe you decided that you needed to do all this with intentionality and purpose and unwavering devotion to see a change in yourself, to see a change in the world.

I suspect that you're reading this book because you have decided that this new antiracist journey you have embarked on cannot be a fleeting thought or a passing interest. You're probably reading this book because you genuinely want to be part of the movement, the struggle, the change. You undoubtedly want to be more than just an ally—you want to be an advocate, an accomplice, a co-conspirator. Perhaps you see your own liberation, and everyone's liberation—not just the liberation of Black people and other oppressed and marginalized people—as tied together, as all part of the same "we," as essential to the elevation and celebration of Black humanity, and all humanity. You're likely reading this book because you are looking for ways to optimize your impact, increase your cultural fluency, and be the change you want to see in the world. You probably want to model curiosity and humility and courage so you can inspire others to model curiosity and humility and courage. You probably see yourself emerging as a change agent, a disrupter, a status quo buster who wants to drive conversations and impact and transformation, who wants to inspire others to do better and to be better.

And because of this dedication and commitment, because of this fundamental change in yourself, you undoubtedly realize that this book will not be the only book you read on antiracism, but one of the dozens of books to read and reference and consult and share with others. You likely have a clear understanding that reading one book on antiracism will never be enough on its own to make a difference, that this book will be one small part of your ongoing and lifelong antiracism journey. And you, of course, understand that because the author of this book is a White male—with all the privileges that come with being a White male—that he should not be your only inspiration.

He should not be viewed as an authority on race or racism. He is not an expert on race or racism. He, like you, has not had the lived experiences that Black and other people of color have had. Therefore what he has to say and the perspectives he shares are limited. And, you doubtless also recognize that for racism to have any chance of ending, for the systems to be dismantled, you and the author and billions of White people need to play an active part in the dismantling of that system, in ending racism.

Ultimately, you're probably reading this book because you no longer want to be that person. That person who doesn't know, doesn't care, and doesn't have anything to say, doesn't want to get involved, doesn't recognize nuances or appreciate subtleties, and doesn't see reality because you have chosen not to see reality.

I can imagine you are reading this book because you care deeply about humanity—your own and others'.

Suggestions for How to Read This Book

You can read the book straight through or you can jump around to whatever sections or pieces interest or move you. Each section consists of a longer introduction followed by several shorter vignettes, and ends with a few questions inviting you to reflect. Each vignette stands on its own. And the book is structured intentionally by themes. There is a flow that unfolds a story that reveals more about me and my humanity, about you and your humanity, about us and our collective humanity.

I encourage you to underline, highlight, annotate, write in the margins, dog-ear, and discuss individual introductions or vignettes or the entire book with others. Flag with stickies the parts that resonate. Come back and reread them. Use the unique pieces as pre-reads or post-reads in team meetings, offsites, or company trainings. Begin discussions, conversations, and explorations to answer the reflection questions at the end of each section. Start reading groups, contemplate, think deeply, invite me into your company to elaborate or clarify or inspire or coach. Use this book as an ongoing resource, a companion in your continued personal and professional and social and antiracist development.

I hope as you read this book you will reflect and question and allow yourself to feel whatever you're feeling. I hope you will identify and validate those feelings. I hope you will sit with your uncertainty and observe your emotions and engage your imagination and let yourself wonder. Stay present through all the parts that make you uncomfortable and the parts you don't understand, the parts you are unfamiliar with, disagree with, think you disagree with, the parts that challenge your perception of yourself, your behaviors, your thoughts, your friends, your family, your colleagues, your communities, the world, White people.

As you read, you will be reminded that the personal is universal. Even though the specific experiences and incidents and events and stories I share are unique to me, I trust that you will see yourself in my stories. That what has happened to me, and what has shaped me, has in some small or large way happened to you and shaped you too.

This is not a "how to" book. This book does not claim to have all the answers. This book will not solve all your—or anyone's—problems. This book will not dismantle any systems. This book will not make you antiracist. This book is not a panacea for ending racism. What this book will do is challenge you to reflect on who you've been, who you are, and who you want to become. This book will invite you to examine your views and check your privilege. This book will encourage you to evolve your consciousness and commit to continuing your antiracist journey with purpose and resolve. This book will offer perspectives, philosophies, and frameworks to adopt, principles and values for you to embody.

And, if you choose to consider these perspectives, to adopt these philosophies and frameworks, to embody these principles and values, "what to do" will emerge on its own. As you reflect on how this book relates to you and your personal, authentic antiracist journey, you will be compelled to act in ways that are relevant and meaningful. You will implement ideas and practices in your own life. You will share the contents of this book with others. You will challenge others to adopt the perspectives and philosophies and frameworks and principles and values. You will invite others into conversations.

You will become a change agent.

You will demand that others do better.

You will become a committed antiracist.

You will become a champion of humanity.

SECTION 1

My Approach to Confronting Racism

The Devolution of the
Two-Man Book Club

"To know what is right and not to do it
is the worst cowardice."
Confucius

My friend and I had this idea. In 2004, after we stumbled into discovering we had opposing political views, we became curious to explore each other's perspectives. We started a two-man book club. He selected a book. We discussed. I selected a book. We discussed. Since our political differences had not been an issue in our friendship, this seemed a straightforward approach to expand our understanding of one another, and to dive deeper into less familiar perspectives.

But before we finished the first book, the idea devolved quickly. Did he seriously believe what the author was espousing? How could he not see that those theories about class and race were total bullshit? Come on, man, do you really think like this? Do you have no integrity? And vice versa for the book I selected. Our good-natured idea to get to know each other's political views immediately turned fractious, aggressive, mean. Our email exchanges and phone calls were filled with snark, sarcasm, and ad hominem attacks. Unfiltered opinions from partisan sources became the norm. Our conversations in person were more civil but only because we were embarrassed by our behavior. Like trained actors, we played our roles cordially and masked our bitterness with fake smiles, our resentment with acquiescent nods.

We made it through four books. Did we learn from each other? No. Did we treat each other with respect? No. Did we validate each other's point of view? No. Did we drive our friendship bus off a cliff into the rocky canyon below? Absolutely. For three years, we didn't talk. Our righteousness and stubborn pride prevented us from self-reflecting and seeing the bigger picture; from growing and learning and being open to new ideas and possibilities. Our little experiment changed nothing and no one. Neither of us felt good or advanced our thinking. We made no positive impact in the world.

The two-man book club debacle was a huge turning point for me. I started to see patterns in how I expressed my views, not just with my book club partner, but also with almost everyone, and most of the time. My approach and my behavior were not unique to this experience. It was who I was. And who I was, was ineffective because I was so wrapped up in what I thought my point of view was.

In the narrow view of my friend's and my relationship, the two-man book club was an unqualified failure. But in the wider view, I now see that it was another catalyst for greater self-awareness, appreciation for nuance and context, and hyper-focused intentionality around how I was going to approach my antiracism work. I made a deeper commitment to trying to *get* it right instead of trying to *be* right.

I realized that confronting racism isn't about yelling and screaming and proving someone wrong so that I could be proven right. Confronting racism isn't about pointing to a passage in a book and saying I told you so. Confronting racism isn't about appearing antiracist on social media. Confronting racism isn't about winning. Confronting racism is about driving impact and affecting change. Confronting racism is about evolving our consciousness so that we can see which systems need dismantling, understand why those systems need dismantling, and recognize what our role is in dismantling those systems. In the end, confronting racism is about ending racism. Period. Each of us has to do the work to understand what that confrontation looks and feels like and how it gets put into action.

I also began to realize that I should not attempt or expect to reach everyone. The people I am going to reach are the people who are interested in being reached. To change the world, I don't have to save the world. My role is not to end racism by myself, but to contribute meaningfully and consistently to a larger collective of people working to end racism.

There's no antiracism formula or template that I can or will provide for you to co-opt as your own. I can provide approaches that have worked for me, and I will invite you to consider if they might also work for you. The vignettes in this section capture my approach to confronting racism. I have practiced these approaches, honed these philosophies, and evolved these perspectives over the years, and they have become foundational pillars for how I choose to confront racism. They illustrate what I have learned from the two-man book club experience and other similar experiments.

In case you're wondering, my book club partner and I eventually did recover. We're still friends today. And, of course, I still share my views. I'm just no longer willing to be a jerk about them. With him or with anyone else.

Author's Note on Structure and Flow

Each section of the book opens with a narrative essay (like the one you just read). A series of shorter vignettes follows these essays, and each section closes with a few reflection questions. Each vignette can and does stand on its own. That said, the collection of vignettes are perspectives that are related to the title of the section, framed by the opening piece.

The Danger of a Single Story

"The single story creates stereotypes, and the problem with stereotypes is not that they are untrue, but that they are incomplete. They make one story become the only story."

– Chimamanda Ngozi Adichie

Over the last twenty years, I have evolved my consciousness along two entwined journeys of development.

The personal development journey—rooted in mindfulness, presence, self-awareness, equanimity. Grounded in empathy, curiosity, possibility, connection.

And the cultural fluency journey—based in social justice, inclusion, equity.

Reading. Learning. Listening. Expanding my normal. Immersing in new social, cultural, political, and professional situations. Stretching my appreciation and understanding of others' lived experiences.

These threads of development—while unique and separate—overlap and interconnect regularly. They form a more dynamic, more authentic, more complete representation of who I am.

You, too, have multiple storylines that make up who you are.

Sometimes they may be difficult to reconcile. Sometimes they feel at odds. Sometimes there is tension. Sometimes a single action is criticized by one person and praised by another.

The work is to stay on the path. To honor the totality of the journey.

So we can find true belonging. For ourselves. And for others.

I Wrote This Book Because
I Care About Humanity

I wrote this book not because of my ego.

I wrote this book not because it's cathartic.

I wrote this book not because I'm a writer.

I wrote this book not because I'm an expert.

I wrote this book not because I have verbal diarrhea.

I wrote this book not to establish thought leadership.

I wrote this book not because I'm narcissistic.

I wrote this book not because I'm bored.

I wrote this book not as a form of therapy.

I wrote this book because I have something to say.

I wrote this book because the something I have to say is the something someone needs to read at the exact time I say it and they read it.

I wrote this book because I value human connection, and I know others value human connection, and I know I add to the collective human connection by sharing.

I wrote this book to start conversations, spark discussion, encourage dialogue.

I wrote this book to offer unique perspectives, challenge the status quo, and advocate for people who are marginalized.

I wrote this book because I believe more public vulnerability can address our biggest racial, social, cultural, and political problems.

I wrote this book to serve others.

I wrote this book because I care about humanity.

Interconnected Lenses

I view my work through four distinct yet interconnected lenses:

1. Social justice.

Shit ain't equitable. The playing field is not level. It's not a meritocracy. I work to change that.

My default position is to advocate for the underdog, the marginalized, the "onlys."

I resist White solidarity, challenge dominant narratives, disrupt the status quo.

2. Emotional Intelligence.

This work takes self-awareness. Driving impact requires centering empathy, curiosity, vulnerability.

Constant self-reflection. Willingness to change. Cultural humility and agility. Holding space. Okay not being right.

3. Mindfulness.

If we are unable to sit with uncertainty, we're in big trouble. Remembering that we are not our emotions and feelings and thoughts.

Observing without judging or reacting. Striving for a state of equanimity. Detached from my views and dispassionate in how I express them.

So I can stay present and work for the long haul.

4. Storytelling.

My story. Your story. Our collective story. Whose stories are being told. Whose aren't. And why.

Amplifying voices, optimizing messaging. Challenging false and misleading narratives. Uplifting underrepresented ones.

Having a clear understanding of who I am, what I believe in, and why it matters. So that I can help others do the same.

It All Begins with Curiosity

For me, the work begins with being genuinely curious about the lives of other people.

I'm curious about the history and culture and lived experiences of other people.

Individual people I know. People I consider friends. People I work with. People I connect with online.

Individual people I don't know. Musicians whose tunes I groove to. Writers whose stories I absorb. Artists whose creativity inspires me. Speakers whose words move me. Politicians whose policies motivate me.

Social justice and antiracism and equity and diversity and inclusion and belonging work require that you learn industry best practices and know your history and understand systems of oppression and familiarize yourself with many other nuances and subtleties.

And if you're not curious about the lives of other people—how they live, how they hurt, how they love, how they grow, how they navigate the world.

How they're different from you. How they're not.

If you're not curious about the vast dynamism of the human condition.

If you don't center empathy and compassion and connection and love.

Then are you really doing the work?

I find the more curious I am about other people, the more curious I am about myself.

Who am I? Why do I care? What drives me? What keeps me centered? Who might I become?

It all begins with curiosity.

Mindfulness Is at the Core of My Work

My mindfulness practice is at the core of my work.

It centers me, allows me to think clearly, and puts me in a mental state to make important decisions.

It provides me with the foundation to write compellingly, absorb criticism and dissent with equanimity, and engage in dialogue with civility.

It helps me stay curious and eager. Empathetic and compassionate. Available, aware, and present.

It provides me with the space I need to be intentional with my actions and my words and my thoughts. To pause. To listen. To slow down.

Mindfulness reminds me that I'm not trying to be right, win, or be better than anyone else.

It sets the stage for me to influence and persuade and uplift and amplify and collaborate.

It gives me the courage to be authentic. To speak my mind. To say and think and do what needs to be said and thought and done. To lead.

Mindfulness is the conduit that connects me to myself, and the core of my connection with others.

It keeps me grounded, calm, focused, alive.

It reminds me that love and kindness and wisdom are intertwined, interconnected, and essential.

Mindfulness gives me the resolve to make just what is unjust. Equitable what is inequitable. To include who is excluded.

Mindfulness is at the core of my sense of belonging.

Bringing Me Back to Humanity

I do the work I do to elevate humanity—my own and others'.

I engage in dialogue, so I can experience the humanness of other people.

So I can have the privilege of hearing their stories, their troubles and joys, their losses and successes, their anger and happiness, their despair and hope.

So I can hear their journey. And so I can share mine.

So we can connect. And build a relationship. A friendship. A partnership. A trust. A collaboration. A support network. A coalition of collective good.

I center empathy and kindness and compassion and curiosity and equanimity. I stay present with another person's truth. I listen. I validate their lived experiences. I amplify their voice.

I use my power and privilege and influence to make positive change.

Intentionally.

I don't always get it right. Don't always sustain the effort. Sometimes I slip up. Get it wrong. Am inauthentic. Make an error of emphasis. Succumb to incivility. Forget what guides me. Devolve.

But I always get back on track. I always find some person or some message or some experience that brings me back to humanity.

That brings me back to focus. That brings me back to forward momentum and progress.

That brings me back to the vast dynamism of the human condition.

That brings me back to love.

Who Has the Power and
What Are They Doing with It?

If you fail to see that antiracism work is social justice work, then your antiracism work will fail.

I used to be a sixth-grade social justice teacher. The one throughline that guided every assignment, project, lesson, discussion?

"Who has the power and what are they doing with it?"

Are people in power using their power *over* others to control, oppress, abuse, and dehumanize them?

Or are people in power sharing their power *with* others to uplift, amplify, support, and empower them?

Every single relationship in the history of humanity has a power dynamic. One person always has more power in any given context.

It's a choice how they use their power. Every. Single. Time.

From ancient history to two minutes ago, power is either being abused and weaponized or recognized as a force for equity and justice.

Power is either used to create socially just and antiracist laws, policies, norms, realities for everyone.

Or, it is used to continually perpetuate social injustice and racism by suppressing the rights, agency, and opportunities of specific people from already marginalized groups.

Until people in power are willing and able to consistently and intentionally use their power for good, nothing will change.

And we will continue to live in a socially unjust world.

So, what are you doing with *your* power?

Defining Myself for Myself

"If I didn't define myself for myself, I would be crunched into other people's fantasies for me and eaten alive."

– Audre Lorde

I am a seeker. A relationship builder. A creative collaborator. A thought partner. A team player.

I thrive when I'm around other people. Off the energy they give me. And the energy I give them. And the energy we give each other.

I need support. I want support. I want to run my ideas by people. And I want to have people run their ideas by me.

I am a social being. An extrovert. Happy to have a conversation with just about anyone on any topic at any time.

I love to explore and reflect and evolve and grow and discover and understand what makes each person unique.

I seek out discussion and dialogue and exchange and good company and kindred spirits.

I am influenced by other people. Their ideas and their written words and their spoken words and their truths and their lies and their mistakes and their profundities.

I welcome it all and I absorb it all and I use it all in a myriad of ways that are both definable and indefinable. Visible and invisible.

I rely on the warmth and love and empathy and compassion of other people to survive.

And, in the end, I define myself for myself. I am unapologetically me.

And I have not been eaten alive.

Conflating Dialogue with Debate

Part of the challenge of confronting difficult topics like systemic racism and social injustice and White supremacy and other uncomfortable truths is that we conflate dialogue with debate.

We often don't make our intentions clear—to ourselves or others.

When we debate, we try to win the argument, prove a point, establish our rightness or our righteousness.

When we dialogue, on the other hand, we aim to introduce perspectives into a conversation, and we invite others to share their views.

In a dialogue, we can still challenge those views, and we can still offer countering perspectives, but we are genuinely interested in learning from the other person, from the interaction, and from the experience of having a dialogue.

We often go into debate mode because we are insecure, or because we lack fluency, or because we're not interested in the topic, or because we're *really* interested in the topic.

It's perfectly fine to go into debate mode if, in fact, we intend to go into debate mode.

We have to understand that we will get a different outcome in debate mode than in dialogue mode.

One is not right and the other wrong. One is not better than the other.

We need to pay more attention to the difference.

Always with Compassion

I always aim to treat people with compassion.

Even the people who disagree with me.

Even the people who attack me.

Even the people who say and do and think things that are harmful and ignorant and dishonest.

I tell the racist he's a racist.

I tell the sexist he's a sexist.

I tell the homophobe he's a homophobe.

With compassion.

I write and speak and coach and train and dialogue for equity and inclusion and justice.

I call people on their shit. I object to bigotry and discrimination and prejudice.

With compassion.

I share my perspectives even if they're not popular, even if I'm not "supposed" to, even if people don't want to hear them.

With compassion.

I challenge the status quo. I disrupt bro culture. I question the dominant narrative. I decline the invitation to cuddle in the arms of "people like me."

I confront power and privilege.

With compassion.

None of this is contradictory. I am in alignment. I am centered. Grounded. Equanimous. Confident. Competent.

I come from a place of love. Not from a place of fear. Or hate.

I seek connection. I establish trust. I cultivate relationships. I build bridges over chasmic canyons to reach a shared understanding.

I am curious. Empathetic. Always learning and growing and teaching and collaborating.

Always with compassion.

Moving Beyond the Bomb-Throwing Stage of the Revolution

"Some people get so absorbed in expressing their own opinions that they lose sight of how they affect others." – Adam Grant

I used to be a jerk. Self-righteous. Sarcastic. Acerbic.

Firmly rooted in the bomb-throwing stage of the revolution.

I was so attached to my perspectives and ideas that when I hurled them at others with vitriol a part of me was hurled too.

People were put off. People didn't listen. People didn't care what I thought. I was ineffective.

I was easily dismissed, scoffed at, ignored, mocked, condescended to. Which made me push ahead with the same approach with more vigor and determination.

More bitterness. More resentment.

I took this approach for a good seven or eight years.

But I don't go about it that way anymore.

I've come to realize that I took this approach because I was insecure. Immature. Undeveloped. Not grounded in my articulated values and principles. I was winging it most of the time.

I was excited and politicized by what I was learning, and before I let the knowledge sink in and become part of my essence, I threw it indiscriminately at others like a monkey flings its shit at the zoo.

Now, I'm much more effective. I still care just as much. I still have strong opinions.

I'm more mindful of how I might be received.

Self-Actualization Alone Is Not Enough

"No level of individual self-actualization alone can sustain the marginalized and oppressed. We must be linked to collective struggle, to communities of resistance that move us outward, into the world." – bell hooks

In my work helping folks from the dominant narrative do their part to create equitable, antiracist, and inclusive cultures of belonging, I stress the dual journeys of personal development and cultural fluency.

To drive impact and affect change you must be on a continual path toward self-actualization—understanding who you are, why you care, what you value, and how you show up.

And, as bell hooks says, this journey cannot be undertaken in isolation. What good is your self-actualization if it is self-serving, disconnected from the lived realities and experiences of others?

If you genuinely care about the marginalized and oppressed you will also commit to strengthening your cultural fluency.

You will learn, read, listen, watch, grow, immerse yourself in contexts and environments that are beyond your comfort zone.

You will do this without being asked, prompted, or told.

You will elevate your cultural fluency because your power and privilege are too great to go unrealized.

You will elevate your cultural fluency because the world demands that you do.

Writing Makes Me Infinite

"Reading would make me brilliant, but writing would make me infinite." – Gabby Rivera

I finish one book and I go put it on the bookshelf. I pick up a new book and begin reading.

It's like chain-smoking but without the lung cancer and the yellow fingernails and the hoarse voice and the early death.

I don't always write about what I read, but what I write emerges from what I read.

What I write is what I write because I read.

Reading makes me informed. Reading makes me inspired. Reading makes me knowledgeable. Reading makes me worldly. Reading makes me curious, empathetic, compassionate.

Reading makes me brilliant.

Reading gives me ideas: what to write about, how to write it, who to write it for, where to write it.

Writing makes me free. Makes me interesting. Makes me relevant. Makes me unique. Makes me strong. Makes me authentic. Makes me compelling. Makes me feel like I belong.

Writing builds connections and relationships. Writing opens doors. Writing leads to opportunities. Writing makes me smile and laugh and cry and believe.

Writing allows me to express myself. To share my emotions and feelings and opinions and perspectives. To change the world.

Writing makes me proud and happy and powerful. Writing motivates me to do better, to be vulnerable, to be me.

Writing makes me infinite.

The Alternative Is Silence

As a cisgender, straight, White male doing antiracism, social justice, and equity work, absorbing criticism, skepticism, and cynicism is high on my list of skills.

After all, who is this cis person to talk about transgender issues? If I were trans, I'd have doubts about myself.

Who is this straight person to be a vocal advocate for gay and lesbian rights? What the hell do I know about what it means to be gay?

And, who is this White dude to be carrying on about the Black experience? The guy who's as white as snow!

And, here's another man coming to save all the women from marginalization.

All of these (and more) are valid perspectives. I would be a fool to dismiss them. And I would lose my effectiveness.

I put myself out there. I show up. I listen. I speak and write and persuade and argue and try to influence.

And because I put myself out there, there are times when I make mistakes, when I miss nuances and subtleties, when I misrepresent facts, when I'm misinterpreted and misperceived, and when I'm flat out wrong.

My intentions aren't always in line with the impact of my words, thoughts, and actions.

And this is okay. As long as I'm humble enough to listen and learn and commit to improving.

The alternative is silence. And then I'd be complicit.

The Beauty That Comes from Truth Telling

The beauty that comes from truth-telling is stronger than the ugliness that comes from lying.

The beauty that comes from compassion is stronger than the ugliness that comes from judgment.

The beauty that comes from love is stronger than the ugliness that comes from fear.

The beauty that comes from wisdom and kindness and empathy is stronger than the ugliness that comes from ignorance and divisiveness and rancor.

There's a simple beauty in truth-telling.

A trust, an integrity, a humility. A quiet power.

A clarity of purpose. A lucidity of conscience. A fortitude that is difficult to dissolve.

A calmness in the face of chaos. A serenity untroubled by spite. An equanimity that dispels anxiety.

Truth-telling conquers shame, squashes stigma, trounces humiliation.

Truth-telling allows us to sleep at night. Truth-telling provides a platform for deep connections, a foundation for strategic alliances, and an infrastructure for more truth telling.

It may seem tempting to be swayed by hate and dishonesty and falsehoods.

But the beauty of truth-telling is infinitely more seductive, alluring, attractive.

The challenge of course is to be perpetually committed to unearthing, listening to, and sharing the truth.

In the face of myriad forces trying to prevent it from being heard.

Some Thoughts On Humanity

I've been thinking a lot about humanity lately. Not necessarily all 7.9 billion people—but kind of.

I've been thinking about how too often we don't treat each other with humanity.

How we fail to see the humanity in another person because they are different from us.

Or we think they are different from us.

Or we think that what we perceive to be different makes them inferior to us. Not as worthy as us. Not as good. Not as important. Not as valuable.

I've been thinking about why we do this so often and with such malice. With such carelessness. With such indifference. With such righteousness. With such vehemence. With such violence.

Why we use political and geographical and racial and ethnic and sexual and religious and social and cultural and socioeconomic and so many other reasons to justify our dehumanization of other people.

I've been thinking about what we humans miss when we dehumanize other humans.

The opportunities. The relationships. The love. The connection. The collaboration. The trust. The compassion. The empathy. The joy. The belonging.

I know when I talk like this, I may sound naive, or woo-woo, or that I'm describing a utopian world that can never exist.

But I don't know. I don't think it's that hard.

To see every person as human. Including ourselves.

Gandhi Wasn't Passive

Some of the criticism I get with my approach to antiracism work centers around the fact that I am calm, lead with empathy, am always willing to dialogue with people who disagree with me, and don't get riled up easily.

The insinuation is that my compounding privilege allows me to adopt this disposition, that I don't care that much, that I'm somehow—passive.

Well, that's just a bunch of bullshit, you ignorant motherfuckers. I'll prove to you that I know what the fuck I'm talking about!

See, doesn't work, does it?

One of my inspirations for doing antiracism work is Gandhi. A million passages I could quote, but I think this one is relevant:

"I have never advocated passive anything."

Gandhi says this as the British are letting him out of prison. His captors are surprised that he's not more pissed off about continually being imprisoned for standing up for his beliefs and his people.

But he doesn't lower himself to their way of interacting. He is not intimidated. He is not thrown off track.

The British are bemused, condescending, presuming that because he doesn't yell and scream and cuss that he is ineffective, intimidated—passive.

Well, we all know what happened to the British in India.

Gandhi was not passive. Neither am I.

And neither should you be.

Section 1: An Invitation to Reflect

1. What is your approach to confronting racism? Do you have an intentional approach? Have you thought about it much? Why or why not?

2. What are you doing with your power? Who are you empowering?

3. What are your immovable principles? What values guide your antiracism work?

4. Where have you had success in confronting racism? Failure? What brought about your success or failure?

5. What systems in your spheres of influence are you committed to dismantling? Why? How are you going about it?

SECTION 2

Confronting Racism by Calling People In

The Continuing Re-Education
of a Privileged White Dude

"There are ways we can call people into conversations about White Supremacy with compassion for the fact that we're all in this together. We've all been trained away from this conversation."

– Rhonda Magee

In the spring of 1992, I was a freshman at UC Santa Barbara. To fulfill a requirement, I took an Asian American Studies course. The course description said we would explore how our racial identity affected our relationships within a diverse society. I didn't know what that meant, but I enrolled anyway. I was a White kid from the suburbs. All my friends and pretty much everyone I interacted with were White. It wasn't something I thought about. It was just—normal.

Of the twenty people in the course, eighteen were women. They all identified as Asian or Asian American, including the professor. I was one of two men, and I was the only White person. The professor asked everyone to introduce themselves and share why they were taking the course. People talked about the difficulties of being part of a minoritized group, even though they were the "good" minority. Others spoke about the challenges of assimilation while trying to maintain their individual or group identity. Privilege was mentioned several times. I wasn't listening that closely.

When it was my turn, I told everyone my name, that I was a freshman on the lacrosse team, that I was from El Cajon, a suburb of San Diego, and that I'd had a crush on this cute Filipina girl since middle school, and that I thought Filipina women were hot. I smiled. The information seemed relevant to me. A nice compliment in a class full of Asian women.

There was an awkward silence I didn't understand. The professor politely said that my statement was offensive and attempted to explain why. I was confused and defensive. I had just given a compliment. I didn't get it.

A month later, the Los Angeles riots took place after the acquittal of the four police officers whose use of excessive force in the arrest of Rodney King was captured on video. Much of the unrest was in Koreatown, where there was already tension between the Black and Korean American communities. I was aware of none of this when it all erupted on April 29, 1992. The professor, herself from Los Angeles, said we would discuss the riots for the rest of the course. I don't remember any of those conversations. At the end of the course, she organized a potluck at her house.

The idea was that we would all caravan down to LA to be in community with each other, get to know each other better, and support each other in processing the tumultuous events of that spring. It would be a perfect culmination of the discussions we'd had in class in the last ten weeks, an opportunity to further explore our racial identities and to be that much closer to history. But none of that sounded very interesting to me, so I chose not to go.

As I reflect on that spring of 1992, three things come to mind.

First, it took me nearly a decade to even be aware enough to feel embarrassed about my behavior.

Second, I now understand the difference between shame and guilt—how shame keeps us stuck, wallowing in our self-pity, immobilizing us, its pain leading to avoidance, bringing on defensiveness and denial, which leaves us with little capacity to feel guilt that can be channeled to propel us to correct our behaviors, right our wrongs, evolve our consciousness, and continue to know better so we can continue to do better. Because of my ignorance, I never experienced shame. But I have used the guilt I had from offending those women almost thirty years ago—women who I will never again meet, who I will never have the opportunity to apologize to, and with whom I will never engage in any type of healing or restorative justice—as a driving force for my ongoing work.

Third, I now realize that the women in that class, given a choice to call me out or call me in, decidedly tried to call me in. They saw that I needed direction, a guiding hand, a lot of education, and a broadening of understanding of the lived experiences of people "not like me." They tried to call me in, and I ignored their calls. Not out of malice, but out of indifference. And here's the key takeaway: their approach worked. It took a long time, but it worked. They didn't shame me or mock me or try to discipline or punish me. They recognized that the work of confronting racism in all its forms is a lifelong journey, a journey that I had not even begun and that they were trying to kickstart. And, because instant gratification is too often the only measure of success, it appeared that they had failed. But I'm here to tell you—and if I could, I would tell every one of those women in that class—that their attempt to call me in paid off.

I do antiracism work because I see myself in the tens and hundreds of millions of White people who are early on their journey and need to be called in. I see myself in their ignorance. I see myself in their indifference. I see myself in their fragility. I see myself in their embarrassment. And, while there are times when people need to be called out (as we'll explore later), for the most part, I'm calling people in. If you're reading this book, you're already somewhere on your antiracist journey. You're ready to do the work. You are welcome here. You're ready to be called in. And I am *calling* you in.

Another White Guy on the Journey with You

Dear White friends,

It's great that you're asking, "What can I do?" in the antiracism fight. Your enthusiasm and commitment are needed. I don't have a list of dos and don'ts. Those lists are out there, and you should use them. And, change doesn't happen with lists.

For White people, antiracism work requires evolving your consciousness, fundamentally changing your worldview, and navigating the world through an entirely new lens.

It's a life-long journey.

To drive impact and affect change, you have to be continually elevating your self-awareness.

For me, that elevation is grounded in four pillars. I invite you to adopt them as well:

1. Cultural Fluency.
Read. Learn. Listen. Engage. Immerse. See. Hear. Respect. Believe. Validate. Include.

2. Emotional Intelligence (EQ).
Empathy. Compassion. Relationships. Trust. Connection. Absorb criticism and doubt. Don't center yourself.

3. Mindfulness.
Slow down. Stay present. Meditate. Strive for equanimity. Practice non-judgment. Sit with uncertainty. Observe your emotions and thoughts.

4. Storytelling.
Be vulnerable, transparent, courageous. Develop a clear point of view. Own your narrative. Inspire others.

Thank you for doing the work. Your intentionality, purpose, and conviction are needed.

In solidarity,

Another White guy on the journey with you.

We Need More White People

We need more White people doing antiracism, social justice, and equity work.

We need more White people modeling vulnerability.

We need more White people who are culturally fluent.

We need more White people doing personal development work.

We need more White people willing to be allies, advocates, accomplices, co-conspirators.

We need more White people relieving the burden of responsibility and education from people on the downside of power.

We need more White people doing the emotional labor.

We need more White people to STFU (Seek To Fully Understand).

We need more White people leveraging their social capital and privilege to drive impact and affect change.

We need more White people to stay present in uncomfortable conversations.

We need more White people to lead with empathy and compassion.

We need more White people to be self-actualized and to evolve their consciousness.

We need more White people disrupting bro culture.

We need more White people doing antifragility work.

We need more White people telling other White people to get with the program.

We need more White people elevating their self-awareness.

We need more White people who are antiracists.

White people, there's a lot we need from you.

Are you up for the challenge?

Push Through the Discomfort

You're a White person newly waking up to four hundred years of racial injustice.

Good. We need you. Continue on your journey. Don't get stuck on the "I don't know what to do about racism" track.

You *do* know what to do about racism.

What you *don't* know is how to be consistently visibly antiracist.

You don't know how to be associated with antiracism in a demonstrable public way.

You feel nervous making the transformation. Stepping into the unknown. Taking a risk.

Sure, you're concerned about saying the wrong thing, offending Black people, White guilt.

But you're more worried about how your relationships will change with your White friends.

Jeopardizing the social capital you've accrued with White people who have never known you to be antiracist.

The people who don't see you as "that kind of person." Who will be surprised by the new you. Who may tease, mock, and belittle you. Who will ask you why you're so serious all of a sudden.

Whose friendships you may strain. Or even lose.

You don't know how to navigate this. How to absorb the criticism. How to embody the new antiracist you.

Because you don't yet have the fluency and confidence, you feel awkward, anxious, uncomfortable.

And you have to push through the discomfort.

If you don't, nothing changes.

The More Aware, More Culturally Fluent Version of Yourself

"Black women are so angry."

"I just don't understand Black women."

"What are Black women always complaining about?"

"Why do Black women think they're owed something?"

"Don't Black women know we're post-racial?"

If you—or anyone you know or have heard—have uttered or thought these or similar phrases, you should read more books written by Black women.

Here is a short list of books I've read. You should read them too.

Why I'm No Longer Talking to White People About Race by Reni Eddo-Lodge

Real American by Julie Lythcott-Haims

So You Want to Talk About Race by Ijeoma Oluo

Why Are All the Black Kids Sitting Together in the Cafeteria? by Beverly Daniel Tatum

A Feminist Manifesto in Fifteen Suggestions by Chimamanda Ngozi Adichie

Sister Outsider by Audre Lorde

Eloquent Rage by Brittney Cooper

Black Macho and The Myth of the SuperWoman by Michelle Wallace

White Rage by Carol Anderson

The History of White People by Nell Irvin Painter

continued

How to Be Less Stupid About Race by Crystal Fleming

This is not an exhaustive list. It's a start.

As you read these books, read with non-judgment, anti-fragility, an urgency to expand your understanding, and an intention to radically shift your perspective.

Then, enjoy the new, more aware, more culturally fluent version of yourself.

A Black Man and a White Man Both Struggling to Be Fully Human

"This book is ultimately about the basic struggle we're all in, the struggle to be fully human and to see that others are fully human." – Ibram Kendi, How To Be An Antiracist.

Racism persists because we fail to see each other as human.

We fail to see each other as human because we don't get to know each other.

We don't get to know each other because we think we have little in common with each other.

We think we have little in common because we don't tell our stories.

We don't tell our stories because we don't appreciate the power they have to inspire and build connections across perceived differences.

In December 1970, Dr. Kendi's parents met at a concert in Urbana, Illinois at the University of Illinois.

In June 1970, my parents met in a small house in Urbana, Illinois, a few blocks from the University of Illinois.

Dr. Kendi doesn't know me. Doesn't know I exist. Doesn't know what I do.

He doesn't know we both exist because our parents met each other six months apart in the same Midwest college town.

Dr. Kendi told the story of how his parents met in his book. He humanized himself. He humanized his parents.

He connected with me. Someone he doesn't know and may never meet.

A Black man and a White man. Both struggling to be fully human.

Beginning to Know
What We Have Not Known

"Surely it is the most blameworthy ignorance to believe that one knows what one does not know." – Plato

One of the most worthwhile pursuits in my life has been being okay with not knowing.

Being okay with not having the answer. Being okay with ceding power to someone with superior knowledge. Being okay with letting another person drive a conversation.

Being okay saying, "I'm not sure." Being okay admitting I don't have expertise on a certain topic. Being okay being the apprentice.

Learning how to start a conversation by listening. Learning how to seek to fully understand. Learning how to absorb meaning and context and nuance.

Learning to keep my ego in check. Learning to amplify the voices of others. Learning to exist with equanimity and civility.

When I reflect on the areas of my life where I have knowledge, there was always a time when I was ignorant in those exact areas.

Over time, through radical curiosity and profound empathy, I gained enough understanding in those areas to speak with more confidence and competence.

I hope that as we continue the conversation about race and racism, folks who have not previously been part of the conversation join with compassion, humility, and genuine eagerness to learn.

So we can all begin to know what we have not known.

Absorbing the Criticism

It's important for White people newly entering into the racial justice conversation to remember that they will be criticized.

People will doubt your sincerity, challenge your credentials, question your authenticity, be suspicious of your commitment, dispute your fluency.

They will level ad hominem attacks against you. They will try to cancel you. They will gaslight you. They will be mean and nasty and aggressive and malicious.

People are going to accuse you of all sorts of things. They'll say you're engaging in performative allyship and virtue signaling.

They'll say that you don't know what you're talking about, that you shouldn't be doing this work, that you should shut up and listen, that you can't be part of the solution to a problem that your people created.

They'll bully you and mock you and find quotes to support their perspective.

And, if you're committed, you will absorb all of it. You will consider what's constructive, discard what's not, look up what you don't know, engage in conversations with those interested in engaging in conversations.

You will continue to listen and learn and grow and discover who you are, how you can best contribute, and what you need to keep doing to get better.

What you won't do is quit because someone said something mean or untrue about you.

Deeply Curious On Purpose

I've noticed a lot of White people lately becoming more curious about racial injustice.

They are reading books and listening to podcasts and making donations and following Black voices on social media.

This curiosity is good. Continue to be curious.

And, your curiosity must go beyond the superficial kind to the deep, sustained kind.

Superficial curiosity has limited impact. Requires minimal investment. Is fleeting. Reeks of privilege.

Superficial curiosity sees incidents of racial injustice as if they were an interesting new Netflix series or a new technology.

Superficial curiosity thinks things are neat.

You watch a few episodes, buy a new gadget, and then your attention and interest expires.

Deep curiosity about racial injustice requires more intentionality. It requires examining your motivations, experiences, and evolution of consciousness.

It requires being interested in other people and events and histories and communities and relationships—on purpose.

On purpose!

Continuing to learn. On purpose.

Continuing to grow. On purpose.

Continuing to do better. On purpose.

Committing to being part of the solution. On purpose.

Because if you're not deeply, intentionally, sustainably curious on purpose, then what's the point?

An Unwavering Commitment to Seeing People As Humans

I recently read *Banker to the Poor*, Muhammad Yunus's book about how he started Grameen, the micro-lending bank that fights poverty in his native Bangladesh.

Fascinating story of how it came to be. One thing that stood out to me was his unwavering commitment to seeing poor people as humans.

Humans with possibility. Skills. Needs. Intelligence. Dreams. Desires. Work ethic. Heart. Creativity.

Might seem like a no-brainer to most of us. But sadly, for many people in power, it's not.

"Poverty is not created by the poor," he says. "It is created by the structures of society and the policies pursued by society."

And the mindsets and narratives that those structures and policies perpetuate.

Classism and racism often intersect.

Racism, too, is created by the structures of society and the policies pursued by society.

Slavery. Jim Crow. Blackface. Lynching. Disenfranchisement. Redlining. Police brutality. Sanctioned murder. Prison pipeline. Unfair sentencing...

In our organizations too. Name too Black on a resume. No interview. Not a culture fit. "Diversity" hire. Lower compensation. Fewer opportunities...

People in power need the powerless to stay in power.

To other. To blame. To marginalize. To dehumanize.

Let's reject that philosophy. Let's humanize. Like Muhammad Yunus.

Dig a Little Deeper

Are you a White person staying out of racism conversations because you think you have no relevant experiences to share?

Interesting choice.

What about that school friend you played with in first grade but never invited him to your house because he was Black?

And that friend of your mom's who said she liked her neighborhood because no Black people lived there?

And that high school basketball game when your friend got beat up by a Black kid for wearing the wrong colored jacket?

And did you forget your freshman year in college when you told a room full of Asian American women you thought Filipina women were hot?

Oh, and that time on the 19 Polk bus when you had that conversation with a Black man?

And when you were out of town for a wedding and the bartender learned where you were from and said, "Aren't you the wrong color to be from Oakland?"

Wait, those aren't *your* stories about race. Those are *my* stories about race.

Just the ones off the top of my head.

The ones I've explored and reflected upon and learned from and told in more detail elsewhere.

The stories I use to enter conversations. To show vulnerability and self-awareness and humility.

You have stories about race too. And you need to dig a little deeper to find them.

Be Part of the Conversation

I've said it before, and I'll say it again:

We need more White people actively participating in conversations about racism, power, privilege, equity, inclusion, belonging, diversity, and other myriad interrelated topics we like to avoid.

Our silence is complicity.

Our lack of self-education, curiosity, awareness, cultural fluency, and empathy is harmful to people we don't see and may never know.

Conversely, our advocacy and amplification of marginalized voices drives impact and affects change.

Not too long ago, I received a message from a Black woman thanking me for a LinkedIn post I wrote about the unwillingness of White people to be part of the conversation.

Thanking me for not dismissing her "very real experience."

She was afraid to comment publicly because she couldn't risk being associated with the content.

Some of her clients wouldn't approve, as they "are a bit like those described in your post."

So yes, it takes courage. Yes, it may seem like a never-ending battle. Yes, you'll get trolls and aggressive disagreers. Yes, your friends and colleagues will question you and tease you and wonder why you're doing it.

And yes, you have to weather all of that. And do it anyway.

Be part of the conversation. People appreciate it more than you may ever know.

Antiracism Is a Way of Being

While you commit to elevating your racial fluency by reading books and listening to podcasts and watching films and validating the lived experiences of Black people, you also have to commit to developing your personal antiracist narrative.

How do you expect to continually show up for others when you don't continually show up as your authentic self?

If you're newly committed to racial justice, but not committed to the work of exploring and defining and embracing and embodying your personal values and beliefs and principles about racism, how will you sustain the antiracist effort on behalf of others beyond the present urgent moment?

Showing up for racial justice isn't a charitable cause. It's not philanthropy. It's not transactional, a checklist, a one-off event.

It's a way of being. A way that you have to own and live and believe in.

And that takes commitment. Commitment to individuals and communities directly affected by racial injustices.

And commitment to yourself.

So yes, donate. Yes, march. Yes, write Black Lives Matter in sidewalk chalk. Yes, continue to learn.

But don't think it begins and ends there.

It begins with you exploring and articulating your personal story of why you care about all of this.

And it ends when we no longer have to talk about any of it.

Sustaining an Antiracism Effort

It's difficult for White people to sustain an antiracism effort because it's exhausting.

But nowhere near as exhausting as Black people and other people of color living with racism every moment of every day.

Our threshold as White people needs to be higher. We can't let our privilege kick in and peace out of the conversation whenever we get tired.

Because it's too hard. Because it's too challenging. Because we get pushback from our peers/colleagues/boss/friends/family.

Because we're not sure what to do. Because one person says we should do this, and another person says we should do the exact opposite.

Because we're confused. Because we're overwhelmed. Because we're uncertain how to proceed.

This is all part of the work. We will be criticized, questioned, attacked, dismissed.

Our authenticity will be doubted. Our commitment will be suspect. We will be accused of not doing enough, doing too much, doing it wrong, practicing the superficial art of performative allyship.

This happens to all of us. In fact, it happened to me today. Twice.

I'd be lying if it doesn't make me pause, rethink, reconsider.

Make me ask: Am I doing the right thing? Should I be doing this work?

I do get tired. I do need breaks. I do need to refuel.

I listen. I reflect. I learn. And I carry on.

And so should you.

Section 2: An Invitation to Reflect

1. What is preventing you from being more active in the antiracism struggle? What are you going to do to combat that?

2. Can you think of a time when you were called in to confront racism but didn't rise to the challenge? Why didn't you accept the invitation?

3. What are your earliest memories of race and racism? How have those experiences influenced your life? What impact have they had on the person you are today?

4. What specifically are you doing—or can you start doing—to elevate your cultural fluency?

5. What do you see as your main role in confronting racism and dismantling the systems of White supremacy?

SECTION 3

Confronting Racism with Emotional Intelligence

Holding Space to Share Our Truths

*"Often the hardest thing about holding space
is that it can feel like you're doing nothing."*

– Heather Plett

I was fifteen years old, sitting on my couch in El Cajon watching *Family Ties,* when my dad called from San Francisco to tell me that his boyfriend John had just died of AIDS. He was crying and telling me how distraught he was and how much he missed John and how he couldn't believe he was gone and how much John liked me and how he thought I was a good kid. I was kind of listening, but mostly trying to watch *Family Ties.* I was wondering if my mom could hear the phone call or if my dad and mom had ever talked about this with each other. Did my mom know that I knew that my dad was gay? Would I have to talk with her about any of this? My dad was sobbing, and all I could do was mumble trite condolences as I tried to watch *Family Ties.* I hoped that someone on the show would make a funny joke, or that my mom would leave the room to go to the bathroom, or that the phone line would get disconnected, or that something—anything!—would happen to end the suffering, the agony, the despair of this phone call.

Two weeks later my dad wrote me a letter and told me he was glad to hear me crying when he told me that John died because it showed that I appreciated the gravity of the situation. I never told him that I wasn't crying, that I just had a cold that night and was sniffling. In my dad's time of need, I was too wrapped up in my own world to be there for him, to offer him support, to give him a signal that I understood. To have the courage to be vulnerable. To show up. I failed to show up for my dad.

And sure, it would be easy to dismiss all this as the emotionally immature actions of a fifteen-year-old kid who hadn't seen enough of the world and experienced enough humanity to hold space for his distraught gay father to share his truth. His father who lived five hundred miles away and who wasn't yet a big part of his life and who he wasn't yet connected to in any sort of meaningful way. If only these types of missed opportunities to connect with people and hold space for them to share their truth were confined to the young and immature, and not ubiquitous in adult-to-adult interactions and friendships and conversations as well. If only lack of self-awareness and the inability to adapt to change and the unwillingness to be vulnerable were not the norm. If only compassion and empathy and curiosity weren't traits that were so hard to come by that we wonder if they even exist. If only we knew how to communicate with love and respect and humility and a deep appreciation for the vast dynamism of the human condition. If only we were able to take the perspective of another person, to stay out of judgment, to recognize emotion in others and ourselves, and express ourselves with clarity and honesty and integrity and without shame or embarrassment. If we were able to consistently see the humanity in other people, not only in their time of need, but in their time of joy and happiness and success as well. If we were able to consistently see the humanity in ourselves too. Not occasionally but always. As a default disposition. As a foundational principle.

If we could approach conversations and relationships with people who we perceive to be different than us—people with a different race or class or sexual orientation or nationality or language or ability status or religion or interests or skill sets or political views or cultural norms—with a genuine belief that we are not necessarily better than them, that we do not necessarily know any more than them, that our norm is not necessarily their norm, that how we navigate the world is not and should not be expected to be the way that they navigate the world. If we could bring intentionality to these interactions, to these relationships, to these opportunities to connect and build bridges and collaborate to make the world a better place, a more equitable and just place, a less racist place, a more humane place. If we could dispel the concept of "us" and "them."

If we could recognize and understand and appreciate that just as racism isn't only the obvious, egregious acts of racism—the KKK, White Supremacists, hate crimes, Nazis, lynching—but also includes the subtle, microaggressive things like touching a Black person's hair, or not inviting a Black person to lunch, or being surprised by a Black person's intelligence, perhaps we would be able to recognize that antiracism isn't only the obvious and visible acts either; that antiracism is more than protesting and donating to causes and signing petitions; that much of antiracism is invisible, not immediately measurable or recognizable or applaudable; that antiracism requires that we commit to evolving our emotional intelligence, that we are continually developing ourselves, that we are constantly aware of whether or not we are self-aware, that we embrace vulnerability, that we are intentional with how we communicate—how we speak and how we listen and how we write. Antiracism isn't a switch we turn on and off depending on who we're talking to, with, or about. When we commit to practicing and improving and cultivating our emotional intelligence skills, we realize these skills are useful and applicable not only in situations when we are talking about race and racism, but in *all* situations.

If we could commit to learning how to deal with discomfort with grace, commit to the practice of sitting with uncertainty with contentment, commit to navigating ambiguity with equanimity, the possibilities that would open up to us individually and collectively would be numerous, revelatory, and enormous. Would be revolutionary, transformative, and life-changing. If we welcomed new ideas, new people, new perspectives, new policies, new laws, new cultural shifts not as threats to our established way of being, not as attacks on our personal liberties, not as a challenge to who we think we are, but as an opportunity to explore and to grow and to learn and to do better and to think better and to be better, imagine what that world would be like—for all of us, and especially for people on the downside of power. People who have been and are perpetually, chronically, marginalized, discriminated against, disenfranchised, othered, made to feel less than, oppressed, physically harmed, shot, murdered.

We can and need to do better. I challenge us to find more opportunities to connect. I invite us to be more mindful of taking care of our own emotional needs so that we can be more mindful of staying in touch with the emotional needs of others. Let us commit to cultivating trust, to building genuine relationships, to sharing our truths, and to holding space for others to share their truths. So that our lived experiences are validated, our differences embraced, our humanity celebrated. So that we can show up as our authentic selves. It takes all of us to shift our culture to one where everyone feels like they truly belong. It takes all of us to build a racially just and equitable world. It takes me. And it takes you. To listen. To reach out. To be vulnerable. Because we never know when we might not get another opportunity to connect.

In the dozen years between that phone call and when he died, my dad and I found plenty of opportunities to connect. In the months leading up to his death, I found plenty of opportunities to hold space for him to share his truth, to validate his fears, to sit with him in his vulnerability, to deeply connect with him. And now, more than twenty years later, I'm glad I did.

Uncomfortable Being Uncomfortable

"To not have the conversations because they make you uncomfortable is the definition of privilege. Your comfort is not at the center of this discussion. That is not how this works."
– Brené Brown

We're uncomfortable because we don't have the answers, because we can't solve the problem, because our mothers said not to talk about "controversial topics."

We're uncomfortable because we have a narrow worldview, because we have a provincial mindset, because we have not taken the time to understand and appreciate the lived realities of others.

We're uncomfortable because we take things personally, because we don't know how to absorb criticism.

We're uncomfortable because people who are different from us have different perspectives, because they share them with conviction, because we don't know how to respond.

We're uncomfortable because we center ourselves, because empathy is an abstract concept, because we're not curious.

We're uncomfortable because we haven't learned to sit with uncertainty, because we can't hold space for new ideas, because we're attached to being right.

We're uncomfortable because we don't want to change, because we like being comfortable, because we're uncomfortable being uncomfortable.

Have *You* Changed?

You've probably seen the image?

One childishly drawn person with a smallish heart and mind and just-budding flowers for hair says to a second person with the same heart and mind, only bigger, and fully-flowered hair, "You've changed!"

The first person seems to be upset at the second person's change, nostalgically longing for the familiarity of them as they used to be.

Perhaps the first person is bitter or resentful, maybe even feeling betrayed that the second person has the nerve to be unfaithful to the picture of who the first person expects to see.

The second person's response is, "I'd hope so."

A clear statement of intent that it had never occurred to them not to change, to evolve, to grow, to explore.

Of course they were going to discover their potential. Of course they were going to bring greater joy to the world through all they have to offer in their mature, self-actualized state.

So who would you rather be?

The first person, clinging desperately to the status quo, afraid of the unknown, stifling your and others' perpetual renewal?

Or the second person, always ready and eager to develop, expand, and transform?

I know who I'd rather be. Will you join me?

Tell Me More

I'd like to invite you to try an approach to your discussions that I use as consistently as possible.

Whenever someone shares something you disagree with, instead of immediately counter-arguing, say, "Tell me more about that?"

"Tell me more about why you think that?"

"Tell me more about where you learned that?"

"Tell me more about how you concluded that?"

I use this approach even when—especially when!—what the other person has shared was intentionally meant to be challenging, aggressive, or provocative.

Asking them to tell me more gives them the opportunity to expand on their initial statement, and for me to more fully understand where they're coming from.

Asking them to tell me more shows that I will not be drawn into incivility.

Asking them to tell me more provides them with the opportunity to choose how, or if, to proceed with their argument.

If they respond, asking them to tell me more helps me understand how I might best respond, or if I should even respond at all.

I have found this approach often to be disarming. It shows humility, equanimity, curiosity, and patience. It's not what people expect.

It may be easier to argue with people using "facts" and "data" and yelling and name-calling.

But is it more effective?

Empathy: The Most Courageous Demonstration of Strength There Is

I suspect the reason we find it difficult to lead with empathy is because we believe empathy implies weakness or deficiency.

I have empathy for people who feel that way.

And, it is wrong.

Empathy is perhaps the most powerful, effective, and courageous demonstration of strength there is.

What is weak about witnessing another person's truth?

What is weak about imagining what it's like to be in someone else's shoes?

What is weak about non-judgment?

What is weak about staying present while someone is vulnerable with you?

Empathy is not agreement. It is not condoning. It is not sympathy. Or pity.

Empathy is not an action; being empathetic is a default way of being. When we embody empathy we are more readily able to act compassionately—especially in difficult conversations.

You can deliver critical feedback compassionately. Challenge someone compassionately. Disagree with someone compassionately.

If you embody empathy.

If you don't embody empathy as a default position, then when you have those difficult conversations, people will probably just think you're a jerk.

And I would have empathy for them.

The Intertwining of Curiosity and Empathy

I'm suspicious of people who aren't curious.

A few years ago I was having a conversation with another White person about the impact of systemic racism on communities of color. Out of nowhere, he interrupted me and said, "Dude, I'm just not that curious."

Translation:

"I don't give a shit about what you're saying, or what you think. And furthermore, the fact that you keep blabbing on about it is really pissing me off. Now, if you would just shut up, we could get back to talking about important stuff."

I believe people who aren't interested in the lived experiences, truths, backgrounds, and perspectives of other people possess an alarming lack of empathy.

When we're not willing to spend even the tiniest bit of our emotional bandwidth to more fully understand and appreciate other people, it's pretty damn impossible to build trust and connection—the foundations of a sustainable relationship.

People notice when we don't care. People notice our superficiality. Our narcissism. Our callousness.

People feel our indifference and judgment. And they don't like it.

People notice how we treat them, and how we treat others too.

Curiosity and empathy are intertwined. Effective antiracists have both in abundance.

Believe Everything That Anybody Tells You

I'd like you to try a little thought experiment. Do it for a day, a week, forever, however long you want.

The thought experiment is this:

Believe everything that anybody tells you.

That's it. Someone says something. Believe them.

Your three-year-old says she doesn't know where the wet, stinky, yellow stain on the couch came from? Believe her.

Your direct report says it's hard to be the only gay man on the team? Believe him.

Your teenage daughter says her boyfriend is a good guy? Believe her.

Your biologically female colleague says he feels like he's always been male and wants to change genders? Believe him.

Your neighbor says she didn't cause the dent in your car backing out of their driveway? Believe her.

Your Iraq War veteran colleague says his PTSD makes it hard for him to concentrate for long periods? Believe him.

Your partner says he's going to break it off if you don't change your ways? Believe him.

Your colleague says she was sexually harassed by your boss? Believer her.

The Black father whose unarmed son was shot and killed by the police tells the world he didn't deserve to die? Believe him.

You say to yourself you can intentionally stay present and nonjudgmental in any conversation?

Believe yourself.

We Wonder Why People
Don't Trust Us

In *Man's Search for Meaning*, Viktor Frankl says:

"Between stimulus and response there is a space. In that space is our power to choose our response. In our response lies our growth and our freedom."

This applies especially to empathy.

Empathy is a choice. Every. Single. Time.

In our rush to react, to judge, to conclude, we often choose not to be empathetic.

I've led dozens of manager training sessions on conscious inclusion. I emphasize that empathy is fundamental to helping people feel safe, heard, and included.

I lead an exercise asking people managers to read a first person narrative of someone who has been marginalized, disenfranchised, or excluded.

The people managers write down what they notice about the person's story, then we discuss how they would respond if the person worked for them.

Every single time at least one participant's initial response is to question or challenge the validity of the narrative, to poke holes in their logic, to rebut, to dismiss its seriousness, to raise "what ifs."

I suspect that we fear being empathetic because the uncertainty of what comes after having connected with a person leaves us too vulnerable.

Which is scary. So we constantly close off opportunities to connect.

Then we wonder why people don't trust us.

Imagine All the People

"I can't imagine losing my father to AIDS."

"I can't imagine what it would be like to have my son murdered by the police because he was Black."

"I can't imagine being transgender and not having a safe space to use the restroom."

"I can't imagine how hard it would be to be confined to a wheelchair my whole life."

"I can't imagine seeing my buddies blown to bits in combat."

"I can't imagine losing my job because of COVID-19."

You *can't* imagine? Or you *won't* imagine?

Someone shares something vulnerable with us. We can't handle it, so we distance ourselves by saying we can't imagine it.

We *choose* not to imagine. Because it's safer that way.

It's more comfortable to say something that we pretend is compassion and empathy. But actually is just the opposite.

We fill the air with our words, thinking we're connecting and showing solidarity. But we're actually showing the opposite.

We're uneasy with the emotion of it, the awkward silence, the uncertainty of how to proceed.

And that's exactly where we need to remain. Present. Silent. Available.

You might try something like this:

"I'm not sure what to say right now, but I'm just glad you told me."

We all crave connection. We just need to be better at knowing how to connect.

We're Afraid of Love and
All That Comes with It

We often fail to realize that much of our worldview is based on fear.

We're afraid of the other. People who don't look like us. People who have different lived experiences.

We're afraid of diversity because it threatens our safe cozy position atop the social capital food chain.

We're afraid of vulnerability because people will think we're a wuss.

We're afraid of equity because we're not willing to give up our power or privilege and create access and opportunity for people who have been marginalized.

We're afraid of empathy because it will damage our tough guy status.

We're afraid of inclusion because we're worried what our friends will think if we associate too frequently with "those people."

We're afraid of listening because we don't want to be burdened with all the things we'd hear.

We're afraid of social justice because the unjust world we dominate is too favorable to relinquish.

We're afraid of curiosity because of the uncertainty of what we might discover.

We're afraid of self-awareness because it's easier to be aloof.

We're afraid of humility because it's easier to be a jerk.

We're afraid to be human because that would require building connection and trust.

We're afraid of love and all that comes with it.

Do You Have Something to Say?

One reason why we have a difficult time sharing our antiracist point of view with conviction is because we don't really have an antiracist point of view.

We haven't taken the time to develop an authentic, compelling perspective that is uniquely ours and that clearly states what we believe in.

We haven't developed our voice, unearthed our narrative, articulated our story—to ourselves.

We want so badly to be heard and praised and seen and validated and loved—but we're not willing to be vulnerable and bare our souls.

We haven't done the work.

Instead of revealing who we really are, we borrow ideas and meanings and theories and points of view from others and pass them off as our own.

We conflate being influenced and inspired and motivated by other people's ideas with plagiarism and theft.

And we don't understand why it falls flat—just like everything that's disingenuous, fake, a facade.

And then we wonder why people aren't responding to us the way we'd like them to. Why we're not driving impact. Why we're not affecting change.

We don't appreciate that being influential involves deep self-exploration, ongoing self-reflection on what matters to us.

We don't seem to understand that having said something is not the same thing as having something to say.

We Don't Have to Beat
the Shit Out of Anyone

*"We don't have to beat the shit out of anyone.
We can love everyone."* – Brené Brown

We beat the shit of people because we are insecure with who we are and who we could become.

We beat the shit out of people because we fear others who look, think, speak, and express themselves differently than we do.

We beat the shit out of people because we see the world as a zero-sum game, constantly in scarcity mode, worrying about what will be taken from us.

We beat the shit out of people because we have more money, bigger muscles, more education, a better job, more friends, a bigger house, more power, a fancier car, more influence, better connections, more social capital.

We beat the shit out of people because we are ignorant, unaware, uncaring, full of anger and malice and aggression.

We beat the shit out of people because we lack self-empathy, self-compassion, self-reflection, self-awareness, self-knowledge, and self-actualization.

We beat the shit out of people because it's easier than getting to know them, understanding them, listening to them, empathizing with them, validating their lived experiences, learning from them.

We beat the shit out of people because we think it's easier than loving them.

When we beat the shit out of people, we beat the shit out of ourselves too.

Self-Awareness and Empathy
Help Me Stay Focused

I am rarely, if ever, the only:

The only White person in a group of Black people.

The only man in a group of women.

The only straight person in a group of gay people.

The only cis person in a group of trans or non binary people.

The only neurotypical person in a group of neurodiverse people.

And, if you are part of one or more dominant groups, you probably don't often experience being the only.

There are times when I don't think about not being the only. Because there's no reason for me to think about it. Because I don't feel unsafe, awkward, self-conscious, anxious. Because I don't feel like I'm representing "my people."

It'd be easy to take this for granted. That the world I navigate has fewer obstacles. That people automatically assume I'm "good" or "right" or "normal."

And I'm sure I often do take it for granted.

But most of the time I don't take it for granted. I do think about it. Intentionally.

I notice who's around me. Who's not. Who I'm consciously including. Who I'm unconsciously excluding.

I strive to be constantly aware of my social capital, power, and privilege.

I try to be a possibility model for dominant group members. And an uplifter of those who are marginalized and othered.

I'm not perfect. There's much I can learn and improve.

And self-awareness and empathy help me stay focused.

I Appreciate You

Words matter.

I've changed from saying, "I appreciate *it*" to "I appreciate *you*" when someone has done something nice for me.

One word. One word that makes a whole lot of difference.

One word that personalizes the communication. That humanizes the exchange. That shows an intentionality to connect.

It's a microconnection. I think we underestimate the value of microconnections. The power they have to build relationships and trust and closeness.

Saying, "I appreciate you" is more vulnerable than "I appreciate it."

You're putting yourself out there more. You're taking a risk of sounding too sentimental or intimate or melodramatic.

But it's not any of those things. If you're sincere and genuine. If you truly appreciate the person for what they have done or said.

No one has said anything to me about this, and I'd be lying if I could report any measurable difference in how people respond to me.

No. It's not about that. It's about me. It's about how I feel. It's about the changes in how I interact and connect with people.

But it's not selfish. Far from it.

I'm putting out to the world—and to specific people— the vibe and energy and connection that I want us all to experience.

And I appreciate all of you for accepting that energy from me.

Section 3: An Invitation to Reflect

1. How self-aware are you? What do you continue to notice about yourself, how you show up in the world, and how you are perceived by others?

2. Why do you think vulnerability is so difficult? And why is it an essential trait in confronting racism?

3. Do you generally embrace change or resist it? Why?

4. What role do empathy and curiosity play in your life and in your relationships? Why do you think both are crucial in confronting racism?

5. What makes you uncomfortable about confronting racism? What are you doing to push through that discomfort?

SECTION 4

Confronting Racism by Reflecting on the Past

There's More to Life Than El Cajon

*"You can't change your past, but you can
change your relationship to your past."*
– Michael Margolis

My dad and I were walking down Fillmore Street in San Francisco to see Jimmy Cliff at the Fillmore theater. I don't remember what we were planning to do for dinner, but on the corner of Fillmore and Golden Gate I spied a McDonald's and suggested that we go there. My dad said that there were plenty of other good restaurants in the neighborhood as we got closer to the venue. But I wouldn't hear of it. I had to have McDonald's. It was something I recognized, something that was familiar and comfortable, something I knew would offer no surprises, nothing weird. My dad relented and we ate at McDonald's that night, but not before he cracked, "Jared, there's more to life than El Cajon."

He was referring to the town east of San Diego where my mom and I lived when my dad moved to LA when I was five. The town where my mom and I still lived when my dad moved to San Francisco when I was eleven. The town that was about ten percent of the population of San Francisco and had about one percent of its cultural expansiveness and political sageness. The town where I was happy to ride my bike on the BMX track and play soccer on the local club team and spend my allowance on 45s at Tower Records and Milky Ways and ice cream at Thrifty. The town where it was a treat to eat out at Bob's Big Boy and climb on the giant metallic statue of Bob the big boy waiter dressed in a giant red and white checkered onesie-apron thingy holding aloft a tray with a massive three-bunned, two-pattied burger that, if real, would have topped twenty thousand calories.

The town where ninety-nine-point-nine percent of my friends were comfortably and safely White. The town where I knew or had known a grand total of maybe half a dozen people of color, only one of them Black, and only two or three of whom could be considered close friends. The town where I had exactly zero Black teachers or Black coaches or Black authority figures in my life, which made sense because Black folks made up less than one percent of the population. The town that actually had large Latino and Pacific Islander communities, of which I knew next to nothing about, and had even less interest in exploring. The town that had shaped my worldview was my frame of reference for what was good and right and normal.

The town that I clung to in those first few years after my dad moved to San Francisco. The town I always knew I could and would go back to after a long weekend in a city that had so many new and shiny objects that I found interesting in a touristy, voyeuristic kind of way—but that I never thought I could or would truly embrace. A city with tall buildings and big buses and cable cars and steep hills and homeless people and hippies and drug dealers. A city with Black people and Asian people and all kinds of languages I couldn't speak or understand, and restaurants with all kinds of strange foods from countries I had never even heard of. A city with bookstores and coffee shops and pizza joints and museums and jazz clubs and artist lofts and gay bars and drag shows and head shops and barber shops and t-shirt shops and antique stores and ice cream parlors and taco trucks and street artists and street musicians and street vendors and all kinds of other stuff that we didn't have in El Cajon—or if we did, we had nowhere near as many and they were nowhere near as diverse and eccentric.

And the more time I spent in San Francisco, the more I saw the difference between El Cajon and San Francisco. Over time, that noticing transitioned into appreciating and that appreciating transitioned into understanding and that understanding transitioned into embracing. By the time I was finished with high school I came to love San Francisco. I loved the fact that my dad didn't drive and so we walked or took a MUNI bus or a MUNI train or BART everywhere we went. I loved that you could be in one neighborhood with all its unique charm and vibe, and then walk over the hill and be in another completely different neighborhood with all its completely different unique charm and vibe. I loved all the people who I rarely talked to but began to observe more closely—the business people in their suits rushing back to the office after a dim sum lunch in Chinatown, the hippies on Haight Street who offered me doses and green buds, the tourists wearing shorts in the freezing San Francisco summers waiting in line for the cable car, the MUNI drivers on the J or the N or the 22 or the 19, the shopkeepers in Noe Valley, the construction workers in the Mission, the fishermen on the Embarcadero pier, the softball players in the park at the bottom of Potrero Hill, the sunbathers in Duboce Park, the joggers in Golden Gate Park.

I loved all the different friends my dad had—gay friends, lesbian friends, straight friends, Black friends, dog walking friends, commuting friends, work friends, young friends only a few years older than me, old friends old enough to be my grandparents, friends who were artists and musicians and writers and videographers and college professors, friends who talked about interesting things like books and politics and music and culture and community and travel and racism and social justice and equity and gay marriage and the evils of capitalism and the funky new Thai place on the corner and which band was playing at the Fillmore next weekend and how Divisadero was becoming tragically hip and whose photography was showing at the MOMA and which friends moved to the East Bay because it was less expensive and who got sick from their HIV+ meds and who was probably going to die from AIDS and who had already died from AIDS.

And the more time I spent in San Francisco, the less time I wanted to spend in El Cajon. Even though I was years away from my true political, cultural, and racial awakening, I realize now that those years from late high school through college were priming me for what was to come. Like foreshadowing in a novel, I was getting a peek into what and who I was going to become, what and who I was increasingly ready to become. I saw more clearly that my dad was right, that there was more to life than El Cajon, that that more was out there, inviting me to explore all it had to offer, challenging me to step out of my comfortable bubble, challenging me to listen to and adopt new perspectives, challenging me to become who I was and not remain who I thought I was or who I thought I wanted to be.

I live in Oakland now. I have lived here for eighteen years. I don't get to San Francisco as much as I used to. And I know that between 1984 when my dad first moved there and 2021, so much has changed, and not all of it for the better. I know that the Black population has more than halved during that time, and I know that Black people mostly live in the Bayview-Hunters Point and Visitacion Valley neighborhoods in the southeast part of the city. And in the Fillmore district, right around where my dad and I enjoyed a McDonald's Big Mac, fries, and a shake all those years ago. El Cajon and San Francisco have both shaped me. They're both a huge part of who I was, who I am, and who I am continually becoming. I can't escape my past, even if I wanted to. But I can—and will and do—reflect on how the two places have influenced me. How they've influenced my views on race and racism, my approach to building genuine relationships with people, my love of humanity.

Toward the end of the film *The Last Black Man in San Francisco*, after the main character Jimmie Fales overhears a young White woman say to her friend on a MUNI bus that the city is dead, he says, "You don't get to hate San Francisco. You don't get to hate it unless you love it." I don't get to hate San Francisco, or El Cajon, unless I love them either. I haven't been to El Cajon in more than ten years. Maybe I need to get back there and see it with fresh eyes. And decide if I truly hate it. Or if maybe I love it. Or if maybe it's a little bit of both.

Your Experiences Have Shaped You

What are your origin stories? And how have they inspired your current values?

I grew up with a single mom who worked all the time to pay the bills, and a dad who I only saw three times a year because he lived far away.

That's why I value connection.

When I was fifteen my dad called and told me his partner died of AIDS. While he was crying I was watching *Family Ties* and I didn't give him my attention.

That's why I value empathy.

As a kid almost all my friends were White. I didn't think much about it or seek to change it. It was just the way it was. It was just—normal.

That's why I value curiosity.

One of my first teaching jobs was at a boys' school in a wealthy neighborhood of San Francisco. There were three Black kids in the entire second grade of forty-eight students. Their parents demanded that they all be in the same class.

That's why I value belonging.

I was at a wedding in Portland, Maine. When I told the hotel bartender where I was from, he said, "Aren't you the wrong color to be from Oakland?"

That's why I value self-awareness.

I recently ended a relationship with a friend who knows my personal story and the work I do, yet still persisted with his racist and homophobic views.

That's why I value trust.

My experiences have shaped me. How about you?

Recognizing and Taking Our Opportunities

In my sophomore year in college I took a class on Feminist Philosophy. I walked in the room and saw a male professor.

He said, "My name's Professor So-and-so, and I'm a feminist."

I don't remember another word he said, or anything we studied. I was too blown away, and secretly impressed, that a man could declare unapologetically to be a feminist.

You mean men can advocate for women? Never thought of that before.

The following summer I nervously told my best friend my dad was gay, worried she would reject me.

She said, "Big fucking deal!"

You mean a straight dude can support gay people? Never thought of that before.

A few years later I had an intellectually stimulating conversation with a Black man about the book *Invisible Man* on a bus in San Francisco.

You mean a Black man and a White man can have common interests, experiences, perspectives, and opinions? Never thought of that before.

I was given a choice with each of these experiences: dismiss the epiphanies and continue with the old narrow ways of thinking, acting, and being. Or, recognize them as the opportunities they were to explore and expand and dive into the exciting unknown world of growth and evolution of consciousness.

We all have these opportunities almost daily. The question is: do we take them?

Ten Minutes That Changed My Life

The 19 bus in San Francisco. Leaving Acorn Books on Polk Street near California Street.

Late night. The almost empty bus rumbles out of the Gulch into the Tenderloin. An older Black man gets on at Geary.

And sits right next to me.

On top of my stack of books is *Invisible Man* by Ralph Ellison.

He starts a conversation. He says that the book changed his life. I say my dad recommended it.

The man grew up in Harlem. The art. The segregation. The jazz. The racism. The culture. The struggle. The pride.

I'm just out of college. Visiting my dad. Grew up in the suburbs.

I listen to his stories. We trade anecdotes about San Francisco and New York and music and books and life.

As he gets off the bus, he nods to *Invisible Man*. "Your dad's a smart man. More young White kids like you need to read books like that."

With a friendly smile, he steps off into the night.

I am twenty-four years-old. I have just had my first intellectual conversation with a Black person.

Ten minutes that changed my life forever. Ten minutes that popped the bubble I grew up in. Ten minutes that showed me how much I had to learn. Ten minutes that propelled my personal development and cultural fluency journeys that continue to this day.

I wonder how many White people have had similar transformational experiences.

He Was Nice, But He Was Black

Growing up I knew one Black kid. His name was Hugh. We weren't close friends, but we did play on the playground together a lot.

It never occurred to me to invite him to my house to play. He was Black. He was nice, but he was Black.

I didn't know any other Black people—kids or adults—so he was automatically an "other" in my mind.

In middle and high school I may have had the occasional Black acquaintance, classmate, or teammate. I can't think of any, and if I did, I never pursued deeper relationships.

In college I had some Black teammates and drinking buddies. My relationships with them were deeper and more genuine, but I was acutely aware that they were "different."

I share all this because most White people grew up in similar homogenous communities, with little to no interaction with Black people.

Then, as adults we enter the world and the workforce and bring our limited interactions and narrow perspectives to our relationships with our colleagues.

Our homogenous childhood networks remain homogenous adult networks.

They shape where we work, where we live, where we send our kids to school, where and with whom we socialize.

Unconscious bias training will not change this dynamic.

Either will being nice.

Intentionally expanding our networks will.

Becoming self-aware will.

Not being fragile will.

That's How Racism Continues

Paula was my mom's friend. They played soccer together.

Sometimes after practice, Paula came with us to grab a bite at Taco Bell, or maybe get ice cream or frozen yogurt.

She seemed nice enough to my twelve-year old mind. Tanned White lady. Maybe thirty-five. Deep voice. Laughed a lot.

Sometimes she included me in the conversation, but usually the adults talked while my brother and I did our own thing.

One night, we gave Paula a ride home. We lived in a suburb ten miles east of San Diego. Paula lived even deeper in a smaller town—not quite rural but almost.

On our way back home, my mom said out of nowhere that Paula liked living there because she woke up every morning and didn't have to worry about seeing any Black people.

She said it casually, without malice or contemplation or any further point to make or discussion to have. No one else said anything—in the car that night or ever again. Bon Jovi probably played on the radio.

As a kid, I never thought about it again, but clearly I remember.

Now, I see that everyone in that car was responsible for perpetuating racism.

Paula, the obvious antagonist. My mom, the guilty accomplice. And us kids, ignorantly dragging the legacy into the next generation.

That's how racism continues.

Unless we actively work to reverse it.

Curiosity About the Lives of Dead Black Musicians

When I was seventeen, I discovered some of my mom's old blues records.

I'd been a music kid since fourth grade when I started listening to Casey Kasem's Top 40. In middle school it was New Wave, classic rock in high school.

These blues records were a new world, not just musically, but racially too.

You see, these old blues musicians were Black, and almost everything I listened to was performed by White artists.

Of course I never thought about that as I danced at a New Order concert or played air guitar along with Jimmy Page.

Once I discovered the music of Robert Johnson, Mississippi John Hurt, Blind Gary Davis, Memphis Minnie, Bessie Smith, and so many others, I also became interested in their lives.

Most of them were not professional musicians. They were farmers or cotton pickers or shoeshiners or janitors or maids.

They played music at dances, bars, and cafes, or, if they were lucky, at concerts put on by White ethnomusicologists.

In the twenties, thirties, forties, fifties, and sixties, while they entertained White audiences with their music, they were banned from the restaurants and hotels and bars where they played because they were Black.

Curiosity about the lives of these long dead Black musicians was the beginning of my appreciation of the lived experiences of people not like me.

My appreciation for the vast dynamism of the human condition.

Elevating Humanity

When I was twenty-five, I ran a marathon. A few years on from being a college athlete, I was out of shape, overweight, and missing my recently lost athletic glory.

Living in San Diego, I did my training runs along the Mission/Pacific Beach boardwalk. Even in winter the beaches were crowded and the weather was warm.

The boardwalk was three miles long. For my six mile runs, I'd run back and forth. For twelve mile runs, I'd do it twice, or extend into Mission Bay.

For the longer runs, I'd run to downtown San Diego and back—past Sea World, Ocean Beach, Seaport Village, the Harbor.

After every run, I was exhausted, dripping sweat, and sore as hell. And progressing toward my goal.

I ran for three months, lost twenty pounds, and completed my marathon in mid-February.

Never once on my runs did I feel threatened. Never once did I feel unsafe. Never once was I questioned or stopped or attacked.

Never once was I shot by vigilante racists claiming they were looking for a burglar.

And I didn't die on any of my runs.

Ahmaud Arbery was twenty-five, like me. He was going for a run, like I did hundreds of times.

The difference? I am White. He is Black.

I was seen as a human going on a run. He was not.

Someone asked me recently why I do my work.

I answered: to elevate humanity.

My own and others'.

Rich White People Don't Have Germs

A long time ago I worked at a school in one of the richest neighborhoods in the city.

Top of the hill. Views of the bay, the bridges, the hills in the distance.

Four hundred boys. About three-hundred-sixty of them rich and White.

To get to work, I took the train from across the bay, and the bus up the hill to the school.

I loved it. The reading time. The humanity. The dynamism. The urban serendipity.

A colleague of mine lived in a town on the other side of the city. She drove to work. She would never take the train or the bus!

"All those germs! All those—people. Gross!"

The implication was clear.

The germs from five-year-old rich White boys who have been picking their noses and then touching door knobs and railings and walls and desks and each other...

That's not gross.

And fourteen-year-old rich White boys who have been touching who-knows-what parts of their bodies, and then shaking your hand and giving you high fives...

No germs there.

And the hundreds of other rich White boys touching—well, everything.

Nothing to be concerned about. Move along.

Rich White people don't have germs. They're not gross.

It's only gross and germy when the people are poor and Black and unsophisticated, and unfortunately have to ride the bus.

An Error of Emphasis

One of the best bosses I ever had passed away in 2020, losing his year-long battle with pancreatic cancer.

He hired me for my first editorial job after twelve years of teaching. He showed me the ropes of content management, startups, business 101, working with an engineering team, and so much more.

Every day at lunch we'd talk politics, books, art, writing, travel, pop culture. Endless discussions with endless drops of knowledge on endless topics.

He also was a clever wordsmith. A phrase he taught me that I still use today: Error of emphasis.

It's when someone takes the focus away from the main point of an issue, and deflects to a minor or irrelevant point.

Like when people want to focus on how a White woman had her dog taken away instead of how she weaponized her racism against a Black man.

Like when people want to talk about Black people looting Target instead of Black people being murdered by police officers.

These are errors of emphasis.

Sometimes they're made unknowingly, carelessly, accidentally.

And sometimes they're made intentionally and maliciously to avoid emphasizing what needs to be emphasized.

Don't let your discomfort, lack of fluency, and fear lead you astray. Stay in the conversation.

Don't make an error of emphasis.

Your errors could be costly.

Always Recognizing
My White Privilege

First the red and blue flashing lights.

Then the shrill siren blurp.

Then saying "Fuck!"

Then looking at the speedometer.

Then lifting my foot off the gas.

Then realizing I wasn't speeding.

Then trying to figure out what I did.

Then looking for a place to pull over on a narrow road with no shoulder.

Then finally pulling into a dark dead-end street.

Then a flashlight shining in my eyes.

Then a request for my license and registration.

Then the news that I ran a stop sign.

Then a sheepish, "I'm sorry."

Then a rather polite conversation about following the laws.

Then a mini lecture and a request to be more careful.

Then a return of my documents and a pleasant, "have a good night."

Then a grateful sigh that I didn't get a ticket.

Then appreciation that my insurance rates wouldn't go up.

Never an officer harassing me.

Never an officer getting aggressive with me.

Never an officer threatening me.

Never an officer suspecting me of a crime.

Never an officer pointing a gun at me.

Never an officer shooting me.

Never an officer killing me.

Always recognizing inequity.

Always recognizing hypocrisy.

Always recognizing racism.

Always recognizing my White privilege.

Always challenging White folks to recognize their White privilege too.

Section 4: An Invitation to Reflect

1. How did where you grow up influence your views on race?

2. How homogeneous or diverse were your communities and friendships in childhood, high school, and college?

3. What are your family's views on race? How regularly did you talk about race and racism? Think about race and racism? Confront racism? Have things changed at all now that you're an adult?

4. What role has White privilege played in your life? What are you doing with that privilege?

5. Looking back, what would you do differently in your past if you could apply your current perspective, wisdom, and maturity?

SECTION 5

Confronting Racism With Mindfulness

The Solace of Sanchez Street

"The fact of the shifting, changing nature of our emotions is something we could take advantage of. But do we? No. Instead, when an emotion comes up, we fuel it with our thoughts, and what should last one and a half minutes may be drawn out for ten or twenty years. We just keep recycling the story line. We keep strengthening our old habits."

– Pema Chödrön

In the spring of 1999, doctors found a tumor in my dad's brain. He had been HIV+ for more than ten years, living a fairly healthy life during that time. But the disease had started to catch up with him, and the drugs he was taking to fight it were showing their limitations. The tumor was treated, but he was soon diagnosed with Non-Hodgkin's Lymphoma, and the cancer spread rapidly through his body. On September 29, 2000, he died of complications from AIDS.

Knowing the end was near he sought solace in mindfulness and meditation practice. A woman named Karen Van Dyne ran a small meditation group for gay men on Sanchez Street in the Duboce Triangle neighborhood of San Francisco. It was a beautiful, expansive yoga studio with yellowish-beige hardwood floors and high ceilings covered mostly with skylights. The space was a peaceful, urban sanctuary. When I would visit my dad during those final two years in 1999 and 2000, I would accompany him to the sessions. Sitting in a small circle, each of us on our individual cushion, Karen led us through breathing exercises, invited us to revel in the luxurious stillness, and softly reminded us through meditations on loving kindness of our individual and collective humanity.

I remember these sessions fondly now, but at the time I'm not sure how much I got it. I was often bored and uncomfortable, constantly having to get up and stretch or walk around. The physical and emotional discomfort was agonizing to my inflexible body and my spiritually underdeveloped mind. Which I know now was the point. My entire life I had done everything in my power to avoid physical and emotional pain, and if I couldn't avoid the pain altogether, then I did everything in my power to lessen it or treat it with a self-prescribed medication. Sit with it, observe it, welcome it? Why would I—or anyone—ever consciously choose to do such a thing?

After my dad died, I stopped going to those—or any—meditation circles, and I can't say that I immediately took up any sort of meditation practice on my own. But I did start to read books on Buddhism and meditation and mindfulness. I did start to more fully appreciate the philosophy and ethos of Buddhism and mindfulness. I was fascinated by the concept of bringing my self-awareness along with me wherever I went, so I could always be present to what was going on around me and within me. I began to see the immense value in equanimity, the idea that I could remain mentally and emotionally calm no matter what was happening. I dove deeper into the idea of detachment and began to more fully appreciate the subtlety of the concept, that being detached didn't mean not caring or being aloof or indifferent. It meant not clinging to my opinions and emotions, and not clinging to wanting things to be different than they were. And I started to appreciate the idea of dispassion, how we can all too easily conflate passion with purpose, and how passion can too easily get in the way of purpose. And I started to appreciate that everything was impermanent, and that everything was now, if I was willing to open my mind to the possibilities.

It was in those early years of the twenty-first century when I was learning about and contemplating and trying to figure out ways to incorporate these practices into my daily life, that I was also experiencing my political and cultural and racial awakening. I was reading and listening and watching and immersing, infinitely expanding my world with new ideas, unfamiliar concepts, more expansive perspectives, people from a diversity of backgrounds, and communities that I had never bothered to explore or support or join. As I learned more about the history of systems and institutions of power and oppression and colonialism and capitalism and racism, I became more energized and more committed to social justice and racial equity. I also became more self-righteous, more combative, more argumentative, more sarcastic and snide—more of an asshole. Seriously, how could people not know about and understand and believe what had happened and was happening every day to people and communities on the downside of power? How could they not see what I see, think what I think, and believe what I believe?

Even though I was reading books on mindfulness and starting to meditate more regularly, and even though I understood intellectually how important it was to cultivate equanimity and to observe my emotions, I found it difficult to countenance these two evolving aspects of myself. But over time, as I continued on my parallel journeys of cultural fluency and self-development, I found that my mindfulness pursuits were not only perfectly complementary to my cultural fluency pursuits, they were absolutely necessary. The more I practiced meditation and mindfulness principles, the less angry I became, the more I was able to focus on what truly mattered to me, stay present in important conversations, and be consistently curious and empathetic and compassionate.

But none of that happened right away. The turning point, and the catalyst for a deeper commitment to mindfulness as a way of life, occurred in 2009 on a soccer field on a Monday night in Berkeley. My twins were nine months old and we had just driven the ten-plus-hour drive back to the Bay Area from a wedding in Palm Springs. We got home just in time for me to collect my gear and rush off to my co-ed over-30s recreation league soccer game. I arrived at the field, quickly put on my cleats, ran into the game, and within two minutes I had scored a goal. Or so I thought. The ref didn't see it, and his failure to award my goal was not something I could accept. I began yelling and screaming and cursing, and was immediately shown a red card, which I slapped out of his hand. He continued to blow his whistle and I slapped it out of his mouth, which to everyone watching, looked like I had punched him in the face. He fell to the ground, someone yelled, "OH MY GOD!" and I ran to my bag, walked off the field, got in my car and drove back home, crying for the entire twenty-minute drive. I was still crying when I walked in the house. My partner, surprised that I was home so early and seeing me in the state I was in, asked what had happened. I told her everything, how I was embarrassed and ashamed, and how I had to change. My mind went back to how much of my childhood was filled with angry reactions to things that didn't deserve angry reactions, like when I was twelve and kicked a hole in my bedroom door because my mom wouldn't let me go to a friend's house, or when I was sixteen and I punched one of my best friends several times in the face as I was driving down the road in my truck because he had the gall to complain that Burger King had put pickles on his hamburger. These and other memories flashed through my head that night, and over the coming days and weeks and months I began to more fully understand that my adulthood, like my childhood, was being disproportionately influenced and impacted by my anger, that I had to stop doing this kind of stuff, that I could no longer be this kind of guy. My young babies deserved better, my partner deserved better, my friends deserved better, the world deserved better. I deserved better.

While that soccer game was the moment I committed to changing my life, the moment where I decided that enough was enough, my transformation didn't happen overnight. It doesn't work like that. It's not some sort of automagical flipping of a switch and boom, everything is solved and everything is better and my world becomes a utopian dream of tranquility and enlightenment. Twelve years later and I'm still practicing, still making mistakes, still learning and unlearning, still struggling at times, still growing and exploring and committing and recommitting, still evolving my awareness and consciousness and understanding, still appreciating that there is no end, that there is no arrival, that there is no tangible goal or ticker tape finish line to cross.

And these same realizations are also true to my antiracism work. It's admittedly kind of a cliché, but antiracism work is a lifelong journey. There is no end to our antiracism work until racism no longer exists. Like our mindfulness and meditation practice, our antiracism work requires long term commitment, constant self-awareness, and ongoing reassessment of our impact and effectiveness. If we are committed, we understand that we will regularly struggle to get it right, that we will make many mistakes and learn from each one, and that we will continue to learn and unlearn and learn and unlearn. We will continue to listen and be humble and grow and expand and evolve. We will recognize the times when we are trying to prove that we are antiracist at the expense of actually being antiracist. We will realize that bomb-throwing rarely works, that aggression is only met with more aggression, and that reacting to everything that everyone says or does or thinks takes away from actually doing the work. None of these realizations will happen immediately. They didn't for me, and they won't for you.

On the corner of Duboce and Sanchez, kitty corner from Duboce Park—the park where my dad and I used to take the dogs to run and play while we chatted with the other dog owners—is Duboce Park Cafe. My partner works nearby and I'll occasionally meet her there for lunch. Afterwards, as she walks back up the hill on Duboce to work, I walk a half block down Sanchez to the duplex where the yoga studio used to be. I wonder who lives in those apartments, and if they know that where they now sleep and eat and watch TV and do whatever else they do, was once a beautiful expansive yoga studio. A yoga studio that brought solace to one father nearing the end of his life's journey. And solace to his son at the beginning of his.

If More People Were More Mindful

If more people practiced mindfulness there would be less racism.

If more people were in touch with who they are, what they believe, what they care about, and how they want to be in the world.

If more people learned to sit still for thirty minutes or twenty minutes or ten minutes or five minutes or one minute focusing on their breath.

If more people realized they don't actually have strong opinions on all the things they think they have strong opinions about.

If more people intentionally cultivated an inner state of calmness and equanimity.

If more people responded instead of reacted.

If more people came from a place of stillness and caused less harm with their words and behaviors and interactions with other people.

If more people were self-actualized and inherently valued and practiced empathy and compassion.

If more people were more certain about what and where and to whom they belong and were more able to help foster and build communities of belonging for others.

If more people were not attached to desires and emotions and political identities and circumstances and their ego and the status quo.

If more people learned the difference between observation and judgment.

If more people were more mindful.

Respond Instead of React

"We don't sit in meditation to become good meditators. We sit in meditation to become more awake in our lives." – Pema Chödrön

Every morning I come to the basement and sit in my favorite chair. I cover my legs with the wool blanket from the wicker basket.

I set the dimmer to just a hint of light in the quiet, dark room.

I settle in and get comfortable. On the table next to the chair is my meditation bowl and my wooden stick.

I gently hit the bowl with the stick and close my eyes. I breathe in and out as the sound of the bowl fades to nothing.

The sound of the bowl is replaced by the sound of the grandfather clock, the heater vent, the electricity from the cable box, the car door outside.

I continue to breathe. I don't try to "clear my mind" or "reach enlightenment" or "relax."

No, I am intent on being present with where I am and what is around me. The stillness is luxurious.

I sit for fifteen minutes. Thoughts come and go. Breaths come in and out. I remain still and listen to the sounds.

I do this every morning. I meditate so I can be alive for the rest of my day.

So I can be present in my conversations.

So I can stay focused on my tasks.

So I can be calm under pressure.

So I can respond instead of react.

The Interconnectedness of Mindfulness and Racial Justice

We would all do well to pay closer attention to the interconnectedness of mindfulness and racial justice.

Mindfulness allows us to be awake to the present moment that's happening now and now and now.

Mindfulness keeps us in a state of equanimity, which allows us to respond, not react to racial injustices that are happening and continue to happen all around us.

Mindfulness helps us remember that we are not our emotions, that passion is not the same as purpose, that detachment from our views is good because it allows us to believe what we believe with clarity and commitment.

Mindfulness shows us we are more impactful and effective when we move past the bomb-throwing stage of the revolution.

Mindfulness puts us in a position to influence and persuade with conviction and believability, helps our credibility and validity.

Mindfulness helps us declutter our thoughts, prioritize what needs to be prioritized, and speak and write with precision and relevancy and power.

Mindfulness connects us to ourselves and others, builds bridges across differences, deepens trust, keeps us from going astray and devolving into argumentation, reminds us that debate is not the same as dialogue.

Mindfulness makes it clear that we will not affect change in the world until we understand ourselves.

A Case for Dispassion
and Detachment

People are surprised when I say I am not a passionate person, that I am detached from my opinions.

They're surprised because they see me articulate my perspectives confidently and competently and consistently.

They're amazed because they see that I challenge the status quo unapologetically. That I disrupt the dominant narrative. That I amplify the voices of the marginalized. Represent the underrepresented.

They recognize my willingness to be vulnerable and open and candid. Embody the traits of empathy and curiosity and courage that I want to see in others.

They understand that I don't *have* to do any of this. That I *choose* to do all of it. That I *want* to live this way, to *be* this way, to be *perceived* this way.

They appreciate my transparency and my intentionality and my purpose. That I am driven by clear values and grounded principles.

And they wonder: How can you be and do and say and think all that and not be passionate?

My answer is that it is *dis*passion that allows me to consistently be who I am—to say and do and think the things I say and do and think.

I am detached from the outcomes of my thoughts and words and actions. I trust in their truth and resonance and power.

All passion would do is lessen their impact.

Which would defeat the whole point.

Whatever You Do,
Do Not Scratch That Itch

Try this at home.

Sit in a chair reading a book. Other than your eyes moving across the page, and your fingers flipping the pages, sit perfectly still.

In addition to consuming the words, notice your breathing. Also, notice any discomfort in your body—the slight pressure on your crossed ankles, soreness in your hip, an itch on your forehead.

Just notice your body sensations.

But whatever you do, do not attend to them. Do not uncross your ankles. Do not shift your body in the chair. Do not scratch your itch.

Continue to read, concentrating on the book.

Continue to notice the itch, the sore ankles or hips. Notice if it's difficult or easy to not attend to the itch or the soreness.

Notice if it's not really as agonizing as you thought it would be. Notice when it goes away on its own.

As you continue to read, notice your joy when the itch goes away on its own, when the sore hip or ankles are no longer uncomfortable.

Now apply this patient, non-reactive approach to conversations and interactions with your colleagues and clients and customers and family members and social media trolls and people with whom you disagree.

Notice how it changes your entire worldview. Notice that you have a choice of how to—or whether to—respond to anyone or anything.

Every. Single. Time.

A Big Difference Between Detachment and Attachment

One of the most powerful recurring realizations I have is remembering that I'm not attached to my views.

Remembering that in any given situation or conversation I have the autonomy to respond in the manner that I choose.

Remembering that I don't have to take it personally if someone disagrees with me or the way I've expressed my perspective.

Remembering that just because someone has chosen to use aggressive language or bullying tactics or be dismissive of me or my views that I don't have to match their style or methods or tone.

Remembering that who I am is not the same thing as what I say, think, or do.

Remembering that my goal is not to win an argument or convince someone to change their mind but rather to offer a unique perspective for people to consider if they choose.

Remembering that there's a big difference between responding and reacting, between curiosity and expertise, between empathy and judgment, between equanimity and agitation, between love and fear.

Between self-actualization and insecurity, between confidence and arrogance, between humility and submissiveness.

Between detachment and attachment.

Yeah, sometimes I forget all that. But I try to remember it all as much as possible.

When I do, I get better results.

When I'm On My Game,
I'm Never Wrong

I might be wrong about this. But I'm not really interested in being right that often.

Sure, I have my opinions. And things I care about. And I see things that should be different. And I work to change things.

But I'm not necessarily interested in being right.

At least I don't think so. But I could be wrong.

I'm mostly unattached to my words and my thoughts and my actions being right.

I don't feel the need to be credited with the right answer or the right solution or the right perspective.

I like to engage in dialogue, throw out ideas to start conversations, have discussions on any number of topics, but I don't get into arguments with people that much.

Unless of course I know I'm right and I feel a strong need to defend my rightness.

And that's when things fall apart. Chinua Achebe was right.

When I get hooked into centering my rightness over my curiosity, my entire dynamic shifts. And not for the better.

I close off. I lose interest. I shut myself and shut others down.

When I put all my energy into being right, I'm left with little energy to listen, to hear, to understand, to learn, to grow, to love, to relate.

When I'm on my game, I'm never wrong. Because I'm not trying to be right.

And that's a good place to be. I'm pretty sure I'm right about that.

Fewer Minefields

*"When you run with destruction in your heart,
you find yourself in minefields all the time."*

– Gabby Rivera

About twenty years ago, I did something that fundamentally changed my life.

Whenever I was driving and someone did something that made me angry or cynical or aggressive or judgmental, I didn't look at them.

That's it. That's all I did.

Someone cut me off. Didn't look at them. Someone going twenty miles per hour getting on the freeway. Didn't look at them. Someone failed to signal. Didn't look at them.

Initially, I noticed I'd still get angry, but by not acknowledging the person, I stopped perpetuating a story about who they were, why they did what they did, and how I was somehow their intentional victim.

Quickly, the severity and duration of my emotions decreased significantly until I rarely had negative emotions while driving at all.

Then I applied the same principle to other parts of my life. I stopped judging, begrudging, gossiping, scolding.

And I began to experience an infinite increase in mental and intellectual bandwidth that was previously unavailable to me.

I stopped taking things personally. I no longer gave my attention to emotions and ideas and people and situations that didn't deserve my attention.

And now I live in a world with far fewer minefields.

I'm Putting My Money on Buddha

Back in 2000 when my dad was sick and dying of AIDS, he got more "spiritual."

Which included reading books on Buddhism.

He started quoting things to me.

I was twenty-seven, only a tiny bud of what would become the flower of my spiritual (and emotional and political and cultural and intellectual and racial) awakening.

One quote I remember:

"Learn to observe without judging or reacting."

Not sure if it was a direct Buddha quote, but I was immediately drawn to it—intellectually at least.

I wrote the quote on a whiteboard in the bell closet of the hotel where I worked as a bellman and valet.

As a joke, someone changed it to say:

"Learn to judge and react without observing."

Ha, ha!

It was all good fun. We laughed for a few minutes, and nothing more was said.

And after twenty years of mindfulness practice, of intentionally trying to observe without judging or reacting, I can't help but notice that so much of the strife and conflict and war and divisiveness and racism and echo chambering and hatred and misunderstanding and othering and canceling and...

Comes from judging and reacting without observing.

It's hard to know who was really onto something—my dad and Buddha or the jokesters on the bell staff.

I'm putting my money on my dad and Buddha. Seems like a more worthwhile pursuit.

Making Peace with Ambiguity

I want to invite you to adopt an approach to life called negative capability that I have found helpful in my life.

Negative capability is "the willingness to embrace uncertainty, live with mystery, and make peace with ambiguity."

The poet Keats coined the concept in the early nineteenth century as a rebuttal to society's insistence on definitive answers.

In the last two hundred years its application has expanded.

Take the modern-day example of engaging in difficult conversations about racism, social justice, identity, power, privilege, exclusion, equity, belonging…

Often, because we lack familiarity (let alone fluency) with these topics, we choose to disengage from important conversations that need to happen if we are to make progress.

The root of this fragility is usually fear, pride, or arrogance, all signs of discomfort, which leads to disengaging from the conversation, which leads to lack of learning, which leads to a preservation of the status quo.

Which leads to continued exclusion and marginalization, which leads to distrust, which leads to low motivation and engagement, which leads to resentment and bitterness, which leads to more arguments and fighting and wars, which leads to more racism.

Wow! All that because we are uncomfortable being uncomfortable.

What a shame.

I Don't Really Have
an Opinion on That

I suspect the vast majority of arguments would disappear if we realized that we don't care about the things we claim to care about.

I don't know if it's human nature, or societal pressure, or how we're brought up, or what we're taught in school, or insecurity, or stress, or lack of self-actualization, or carelessness, or immaturity, or ego, or what...

But it seems like so many of us feel the need to have an opinion on just about everything there is to have an opinion about.

We seem to be averse to responding with:

"I don't know" or

"I don't really have an opinion about that" or

"Hmmm..." or

"That's really interesting; please tell me more."

Or any number of non-committal, non-combative, non-egotistical, non-expert, non-aggressive, non-partisan, non-political, non-biased responses that we could choose.

But don't.

Instead we choose to not only have an opinion on just about everything. We have a *LOUD, BOISTEROUS, DISMISSIVE, ZERO SUM GAME, CANCELING, SELF-RIGHTEOUS, BULLYING OPINION ON JUST ABOUT EVERYTHING.*

It doesn't have to be that way. We choose to make it that way—individually and collectively.

All this said, I don't have that strong of an opinion about it.

It's something I've been thinking about a lot, and I thought I'd share.

A Poor Facsimile of Wisdom

Most people are not wise. This is not a judgment or an assessment or a reaction to any recent interaction.

It's an observation.

Our lack of wisdom shines when we are put—or when we put ourselves—in circumstances where we are expected to say something profound or clever or inspiring.

But because we have not spent the time over the years to explore and truly understand who we are and what we believe in and how we want to be in the world, we say and do and think things that are not wise.

Things that are stupid or inaccurate or harmful or superfluous or racist.

Because we haven't cultivated equanimity and compassion and empathy, our minds are filled with inauthentic fluff, which leads to inauthentic fluff leaping off our tongues.

This is the norm, the default, what we have come to expect from our friends, our colleagues, our leaders, our celebrities—ourselves.

Because we lack wisdom we are unable to recognize that what passes for wisdom is anything but.

And we are left with a poor facsimile of wisdom that takes us farther and farther away from truth and justice.

Section 5: An Invitation to Reflect

1. Do you have a mindfulness practice? Why or why not? If you do have one, how does it—or how might it—help you confront racism?

2. What do you find to be the most challenging aspect of confronting racism? What emotions come up for you when talking about racism? How do you address those emotions?

3. Do you ever get attached to your opinions? To being right? To "winning"? Does that help or hinder you in confronting racism?

4. How comfortable are you with ambiguity? What is your go-to response when faced with discomfort, uncertainty, unpredictability?

5. Do you value equanimity? Why or why not? How does it—or how might it—help you more consistently and impactfully confront racism?

SECTION 6

Confronting Racism with Conviction

A Precious Freedom From Choice

"I have nothing personally invested in my opinions.
I'm just, like, inviting you to join me on the
bandwagon of my own uncertainty."

– Taylor Mali

She said, "I think diversity is fine, but we can't have *too* much diversity." And then she and the rest of the teachers in that staff meeting sat around in that third-grade classroom in those too-small chairs in awkward silence as her words hung in the air like a fog, the implicit racism of her sentiment dripping down out of the clouds of White supremacy that we all would have seen had any of us bothered to look up. The clouds we would have recognized as permanent, perpetually darkening our skies and our classrooms and workplaces and institutions and communities and cities and politics and our psyches and relationships and our everything. But no one looked up. We all looked down, keeping our gazes on the rug under which this conversation, like so many conversations about race and racism, was about to be swept.

The two dozen White teachers said nothing. The two Black teachers wanted to say something, but they didn't know what to say or didn't know how to say it or didn't bother saying it because they'd been saying it their entire lives and were tired of saying it and being ignored or saying it and being challenged or saying it and being gaslit or saying it and being reprimanded or outcast or isolated or fired. And I said nothing either. I knew it was wrong. I knew it was racist. I knew more than ninety percent of the staff was White, I knew less than ten percent of the families at the school were Black. I knew the administration was White. I knew they were interested in upholding the status quo. I knew they agreed with the teacher who said that we couldn't have too much diversity. And I knew they were not interested in changing themselves, in changing the school culture, in changing people's mindsets, in changing society, in changing the world. I knew they didn't have the empathy, the fluency, the wherewithal, the courage to change the system. I knew they didn't have the conviction.

And I knew that I didn't have the conviction to say something in that meeting either. And I knew that from then on I would have to find my conviction. I knew I was still early on my interconnected cultural fluency and self-development journeys, and that if I was truly committed to continuing on those journeys, truly committed to learning and unlearning and growing and evolving and making an impact in the world, truly committed to social justice and racial equity and dismantling White supremacy, truly committed to doing my part to level the playing field, then staying silent in that meeting or anywhere and anyplace and anytime I saw blatant racism or covert racism would not cut it. I knew that not speaking up when I knew I needed to speak up was problematic and harmful and racist. I knew enough to know that I could use what I knew to fight for racial justice. I knew that I had something to say, that I had a unique perspective, and I knew that most White people didn't and wouldn't have something to say, that the fact that most White people didn't and wouldn't have something to say was a huge part of the status quo perpetuation machine. I knew that I was going to have to smash that machine, break that norm, fundamentally rewrite that narrative, scoop all that bullshit from underneath all those bullshitters and use it to fertilize new fields where all ideas and perspectives and stories and lived experiences would grow equally and equitably, where all truths would be respected and validated and amplified. I knew that I had to be a model for other White folks, that I had to find more shovels and distribute them to other White folks who could and would and should be diggers for truth and justice and equity, so that they could fertilize more fields, so that they could play a part in the liberation struggle, so that they could be willing and eager and enthusiastic accomplices and co-conspirators for people who hadn't been born with the power and privilege that they had been born with, so that they could use that power and privilege to right wrongs, to drive impact, to affect change.

Without this conviction I would again and again stay silent in third grade classrooms while third-grade White women teachers said smugly that we can't have too much diversity. And I would stay silent in my own classroom and in boardrooms and conference rooms and dining rooms and in all kinds of rooms and spaces and environments and contexts. If I didn't find the conviction to not stay silent. If I didn't find the conviction to think and speak and act on my conviction, on my clarity of what was right and wrong, on my uncompromising belief that all people and all communities and all humanity deserve agency and autonomy and equity and justice.

And as my conviction grew, I realized and began to more fully understand that my conviction gave me a precious freedom from choice, that there were certain things and ideas that I no longer felt obligated to entertain, that no longer needed to occupy my mind, that no longer needed to disrupt my emotional bandwidth. I understood that my conviction was not stubbornness or dogma or self-righteousness but rather a clarity of purpose, an intentional discernment, a grounding in core non-negotiable principles and values. That this conviction was what I needed, and what all White people needed, if we were to stop making all kinds of excuses for why we were not consistently antiracist. Excuses for why we didn't say something or why we didn't do something or why we didn't mean this or why we didn't mean that or why we let that comment slide or why we didn't condemn that behavior. That without conviction, our antiracism was going to be erratic at best and wholly ineffective or nonexistent at worst. That without conviction, White people will pick and choose when and if to be antiracist, and we will continue to do trust fall after trust fall, perpetually closing our eyes knowing with certainty that when we fall back, we will land in the same soft, willowy bed of privilege and comfort we have been sleeping in our entire lives. And without conviction, Black people and other people of color will continue to fall back and crack their heads on the concrete, wondering how they were duped into believing that the people with power and influence would actually be there to catch them and soften their fall.

With conviction, we deepen our understanding of what matters to us and why. With conviction, we can speak with clarity, confidence, and purpose. With conviction, we tell the world who we are and what we believe in. With conviction, we inspire, motivate, and model for others how to identify and embody conviction, and how to share conviction with others. With conviction, we send a message that we are committed, that we are here for the long haul, and that we will not be moved, that the movement will not be postponed, that equity and justice will not be deferred any longer.

I Value Antiracism,
So I Practice Being Antiracist

If you value something, you will practice getting better at it.

If you say you value something, but you don't practice, you don't value it. It's just an ideal.

If you say you'd like to have or be or see or embody something but you don't work to make it happen, you don't value it. It's just an ideal.

It'd be ideal if I was a good cook. But I don't value it enough to practice cooking. So I eat mediocre food at home and I spend way too much money on takeout.

It'd be ideal if I was more handy. But I don't value it enough to practice trying to fix stuff at home. So the light fixture stays burned out and the hardwood floors stay unfinished.

Conversely, I do value being a good parent. I value modeling curiosity and integrity and empathy and respect—traits I want my kids to have too. I practice being a good parent every day.

I value being a good musician. I play guitar every day.

I value reading. I read at least an hour every day.

I value equanimity. I meditate for twenty minutes every day.

I value being an antiracist. I read and listen and engage and interact with people and content and communities every day that help me learn and grow and practice how to be antiracist.

I value antiracism, so I practice being an antiracist.

If I didn't, it'd just be an ideal.

Attached to Whiteness

A lot of White folks are attached to their whiteness.

Sometimes unconsciously. Other times knowingly.

Sometimes secretly, privately, only with certain people. Other times publicly, blatantly, arrogantly.

Don Miguel Ruiz Jr. wrote a book called *The Five Levels of Attachment*.

1. Authentic

2. Preference

3. Identity

4. Internalization

5. Fanaticism

Like our attachments to our political opinions, religious beliefs, sports teams, careers, social circles—everything!—White people's attachment to their whiteness falls somewhere on this continuum.

From level five: whatever it takes to defend and promote whiteness, including killing.

To level one: not attached to whiteness at all.

I think most White people are in the identity or internalization levels.

Where whiteness is very important. We must defend individual and collective whiteness. White solidarity is necessary because whiteness is under attack.

Perspectives, narratives, movements that decenter whiteness are dismissed, marginalized, assaulted.

We see it all the time. White fragility. White people unable to engage in conversations. White people unwilling to educate themselves. White people averse to evolving their consciousness.

White folks must do the work to detach from their whiteness and get to level one.

That's when we'll see progress.

Those Aren't Stories About Race

More White people realize that saying things like "I don't see color" is not only false but harmful.

These statements stem from racial privilege. Racial privilege that allows White people to never see themselves as having a race.

Which means they don't need to be part of the race conversation.

Race is about other people—Black people, Brown people, Asian people. Anybody other than White people.

They have a race. *We* are just normal. If *they* would stop talking about race, *we* could move on with our lives.

With that lens you can see why White people would say they aren't racist. Why they don't think systemic racism exists. Why they don't think they have any stories about race.

Because most of their stories about race are actually non-stories. All the times they didn't see how their whiteness gave them an advantage.

The times they weren't followed in a store. The times they weren't denied housing. The times they weren't harassed by the cops. The times they weren't seen as a threat.

The times they got hired and got the promotion and got the loan and got the good service and got the nice house.

Those aren't stories about race. They're just things that happened. Everyday things. Unremarkable. Normal.

But now some White folks are waking up. Let's hope the rest wake up too.

Actual, Real Live
Black People Matter

To be clear, when I say Black lives matter, I'm not talking about the organization.

Or the hashtag.

Or the movement—although I wholeheartedly support it.

I'm saying specifically that actual, real live Black people matter.

I'm saying the lives of my Black friends matter.

I'm saying the lives of my Black colleagues matter.

I'm saying the lives of my Black connections matter.

I'm saying the lives of my Black neighbors and community members matter.

I'm saying the lives of billions of Black people around the world who I don't know and will never meet matter.

I'm saying the lives of Black people who have criminal records matter.

I'm saying the lives of Black people who are drug dealers and addicts matter.

I'm saying the lives of Black people who don't comply with police matter.

I'm saying the lives of all Black people matter.

The individual circumstances, criminal records, histories, socioeconomic status, behaviors, family situations, employment status—none of that changes my belief that Black lives matter.

"If he would've just..."

...continued

"If he didn't do..."

"But what about...?"

None of it justifies murder.

As long as people justify the murders of Black people, we will need to say Black lives matter.

As long as Black lives don't matter to all of us, all lives don't truly matter.

A Beginner's Mind or an Expert's?

*"In the beginner's mind there are many possibilities,
but in the expert's there are few."* – Shunryu Suzuki

The beginner's mind thinks: I don't know what it's like to be Black, but it's probably a lot different from what it's like to be White.

The expert's mind thinks: There's racism. It sucks. Get over it and let's move on.

The beginner's mind thinks: I'm not sure exactly what to do or say, but I'm going to listen and learn and take actions to fight racism, even if they're small.

The expert's mind thinks: Hey Jim, did we get that unconscious bias training thingy scheduled? Let's do it soon so we can go back to business as usual.

The beginner's mind thinks: I can see how Black people don't trust the cops, even though I feel safe around them.

The expert's mind thinks: Cops have a difficult job. Only a handful of them are racist, but there's nothing wrong with the system.

The beginner's mind leads with empathy, compassion, and understanding.

The expert's mind leads with certainty, stoicism, and apathy.

The beginner's mind is full of love, connection, and appreciation.

The expert's mind is full of fear, impatience, and arrogance.

The beginner's mind is open.

The expert's mind is closed.

So, do you have a beginner's mind or an expert's?

And

"The test of first-rate intelligence is the ability to hold two opposed ideas in mind at the same time and still retain the ability to function." – F. Scott Fitzgerald

It's possible to benefit from White privilege *and* to have grown up poor.

It's possible to have a Black best friend/partner/sibling/ parent/child *and* to be racist.

It's possible for Black people to be wealthy and successful *and* to experience racism.

It's possible to understand that some Black people murdered by police were not perfect citizens *and* to believe that imperfect citizenry never justifies murder.

It's possible to not have experienced marginalization, trauma, racism, oppression, and disenfranchisement, *and* to appreciate that others have and do experience it all every day.

It's possible to value personal responsibility *and* to appreciate that we're not all starting on a level playing field.

It's possible to be critical *and* to be compassionate.

It's possible to have a point of view *and* to listen to others' opinions.

It's possible to do your thing *and* to know that your norm is not *the* norm.

It's possible to change *and* to be authentic.

It's possible to be White *and* to be antiracist.

It's possible to contribute to a more just and equitable world *and* retain the ability to function.

Addicted to Racism?

It's interesting to observe White people clinging to their racist views at the merest suggestion that something they said or did might be racist.

I have no expertise in the science or psychology of addiction, but it kind of seems like addiction.

The vehemence with which people object to possibly exploring an alternative perspective.

The lack of equanimity, unwillingness to engage in a conversation, or do the tiniest bit of self-reflection.

When you're addicted to drugs or sex or power or gambling, that thing owns you. Controls you. Drives every decision.

I wonder if—perhaps unconsciously—racism is like that. I don't know.

I forget who said it, but I like this saying about White supremacy:

When you're used to one hundred percent, ninety-eight percent feels like oppression.

I think we're dealing with some of that these days.

While there are many White folks genuinely awakened to striving toward antiracism, there are plenty doubling down on their racism.

I wonder if, because they've never thought about it before, the recent brouhaha about racial justice is too threatening.

That two percent shift feels oppressive.

And to think it will shift more? Frightening!

So instead of walking away from the blackjack table where they just lost five hundred dollars, a lot of White people are pulling out another five hundred and playing another hand.

Being More Consistently Antiracist

I recently listened to a two-hour discussion on race with Resmaa Menakem and Robin DiAngelo.

A Black man and a White woman sharing stories, insights, lessons.

Dropping knowledge. Dropping mics. Dropping truth.

Being vulnerable. Being raw. Being real.

Connecting. Listening. Creating space. Respecting. Validating. Welcoming. Including. Empathizing.

I took five pages of notes. I could have written a book's length worth of responses and reflections and learnings. I could have listened for another two hours.

My mind absorbing, growing, expanding.

After two hours, they were just getting warmed up. I wanted to grab a drink at the bar and come back for the second set.

So many specific pearls of wisdom that all I can seem to do is talk in superlative generalities.

But here are two.

From Robin: "The forces of comfort are powerfully seductive and allow us to claim we're not racist."

From Resmaa: "'I'm not racist has no meaning because there's no action required."

I'm not "not racist." I'm racist or I'm antiracist. I can admit when I'm racist because I can recognize when I'm racist.

And I can take action. And learn. And evolve. And stay committed. And do better.

And be more consistently antiracist.

White Supremacy is War

"Until the philosophy
Which hold one race superior and another
Inferior
Is finally
And permanently
Discredited
And abandoned
Everywhere is war"
– Bob Marley

White supremacy is Columbus.

White supremacy is all White boards.

White supremacy is colonialism.

White supremacy is four Black CEOs in Fortune 500 companies.

White supremacy is three-fifths of a person.

White supremacy is underpaying Black women.

White supremacy is saying Lincoln freed the slaves.

White supremacy is talking over your Black colleague in a meeting.

White supremacy is Jim Crow.

White supremacy is hiring for culture fit.

White supremacy is the KKK.

White supremacy is not giving credit to a Black person for their part of the presentation.

White supremacy is redlining.

...continued

White supremacy is not inviting your Black colleague to lunch.

White supremacy is predatory lending.

White supremacy is only reading books by White people.

White supremacy is kneeling on a Black man's neck for nine minutes.

White supremacy is losing interest in #BlackLivesMatter.

White supremacy is Karen and Amy and Lisa and...

White supremacy is being offended by the term White supremacy.

White supremacy is White rage, White privilege, White fragility, White solidarity, White guilt, White tears.

White supremacy is

The philosophy

Which hold one race superior and another

Inferior.

What You Do When You're Too Black

You can't figure it out. You're totally qualified for the positions you've applied for—*over*qualified half the time.

But no call backs. No interviews. Nothing.

What's going on?

Your resume is perfect—compelling, thorough, no typos.

Your cover letter is customized for each role—personable, authentic, confident.

Then it hits you. It's your name. Your first name sounds too different, too Black, too African. Probably because it *is* African—from Ghana, to be precise, where your grandparents are from.

Your middle name is less threatening. More palatable. More recognizable. More acceptable. More "American."

More "normal."

So with tears in your eyes, and turmoil in your soul, you change your name on your resume and cover letter, and even on your LinkedIn profile.

You apply for the same jobs. You get call backs within a few days, several interviews that go well, and you land a role that is perfect for you.

Except you can't help but wonder what it's going to be like working for a company that didn't want the African you.

You're excited to start your new job, eager to do well. But the path it took to get here makes you sad and resentful.

You hope it doesn't affect your job performance.

And how will you deposit your paychecks?

A Matter of Survival

When confronted with the reality that they have homogeneous social and professional networks, White people often respond that it's no different from other racial groups.

"All the Indian guys on the engineering team always hang around together after work."

"All the Black kids are sitting together in the cafeteria." (Beverly Tatum)

"Look at all the Mexican [even if they're not actually Mexican] guys sticking together on the corner."

These observations may be (mostly) visually accurate. But what's missing in the analysis are the reasons behind it.

People from underrepresented groups have mostly same-race relationships to feel safe and heard.

They have same-race relationships to protect themselves from the oppression and microaggressions they face daily from majority group members.

White people maintain same-race relationships to uphold the status quo. To protect their dominance and supremacy.

We don't live in a meritocracy. Superficial observations of sameness don't wipe out centuries of oppression and marginalization.

Things are not equal.

Same-race relationships for White people are expected and accepted as normal.

Same-race relationships for people from underrepresented groups are often a matter of survival.

Section 6: An Invitation to Reflect

1. What is your clearly articulated, unique point of view on racism? Do you have one? Why or why not?

2. Can you identify the experience/event/incident when you decided you were going to commit to be antiracist?

3. What does the phrase "Black Lives Matter" mean to you?

4. If you're White, how has your whiteness given you advantages in life? If you're not White, how has whiteness impacted your life? I invite you to make a list.

5. Where do you see examples of systemic racism and White supremacy in your communities and in the world? How are you working to dismantle them?

SECTION 7

Confronting Racism by Telling Stories

Contributing Our Humanity
to the World

"Experience is the greatest teacher of all.
No need for defense if we learn our lessons well."

– Clinton Fearon

I have a confession to make. You know that story I told earlier about the Black man I met on the 19 Polk bus in San Francisco? Well, it wasn't completely true. I mean, it was true that I met him on the bus, and that I had bought *Invisible Man* at the bookstore, and that he got on the bus at Geary in the Tenderloin, and that he sat right next to me, and that he commented on how important that book was to him and how it changed his life. And it was true that he grew up in Harlem, and that we talked about the book and Harlem and San Francisco, and that he said that more young White kids like me should read the book, and that my dad was a smart man for suggesting I read it. All that was true. And it was true that I was excited by that conversation, and it was true that those ten minutes changed my life. But that wasn't the entire story.

I chose to tell you only that part of the story, the part that was a *little* vulnerable and a *little* revealing and gave you a brief glimpse of my world and my journey. But not a full view into who I was and who I would become. I withheld the most important part of the story, the part of the story that contained the real lesson, the part of the story that changed my life, the ten *other* minutes that changed my life. I didn't tell you that after the Black man and I had talked for ten minutes, and after the man shook my hand and said that more young White kids like me need to read books like that, and after he got off the bus and walked into the San Francisco night, and after I got off the bus a few stops later and walked the couple of blocks back to my dad's house full of energy and excitement at what I had just experienced, and after I told my dad all about the experience, and after he was smiling and full of pride that finally his son whose childhood in El Cajon and all that it didn't have to offer was all grown up now and was beginning to have real, meaningful, urban, serendipitous experiences that didn't revolve solely around sports or music or beer, and after it would seem that there was no more of the story to tell, and after it seemed that this story of me telling you about my conversation with a Black man on a San Francisco bus way back in 1997 had no more to offer, right when the telling of this story was about to reach its perfect climactic ending with me being the hero who had crested the mountain and sat at the peak of the person who I claimed to be, and who I have become, and who had seen the limitations of his homogeneous upbringing, and whose mind had shifted, and who has written a book on racism, that's right when the surprise comes in, right where there's a plot twist, that right when I finished telling my story to my dad that night, I said something that you wouldn't expect, or that maybe you would expect...

I finished my story by saying, "Yeah! You know, Dad, he was actually pretty smart."

The smile on my dad's face turned to a frown. The balloon of excitement unceremoniously popped. The air dissipated throughout the room as the stretchy plastic remains of the balloon dropped lifelessly to the ground in a shriveled clump of inconsequence. Up to the point when I said that the Black man on the bus was actually pretty smart, it had almost felt as if my story had been secretly crafted by my dad, like maybe he planted that man on that bus and had told him there would be a young White kid on the 19 with books in his arms, and would you do me a favor and please talk to him about his books, please give him some sort of profound experience, because he's had so few profound experiences. He's got a lot of potential, but he just doesn't get it yet. He's been around so few Black people that I'm not sure he sees Black people as fully human. He's not a bad kid. He just needs to grow up a little. He needs to be in proximity to more than just White people. He needs to be exposed to ideas that will lure him out of his provincial and suburban comforts, perspectives that will challenge him to expand his understanding of normal, points of view that will welcome and invite him into a new more dynamic world. Could you do that for me? I would appreciate you if you did.

But of course my dad did not plant that man on that bus. And even if he had, the experiment yielded mixed results. I *did* have a transformative experience. It became more than evident—to my dad immediately, and to me over time—that I still had a long way to go. That I still had so much to unlearn. That I still clung to my comfortable whiteness like a baby clinging to a blankie or a binky. And that I would have to be weaned off that whiteness, that I would have to cry it out, that I would have to accept that the myths of blackness and Black people that I had taken at unexamined face value were false, that I would have to face some new realities that would initially feel scary, but that would eventually transform me. I can't say I had this clarity that night in my dad's little home on Harriet Street in the SOMA neighborhood of San Francisco, and I don't recall how the rest of the conversation went with my dad that night. But this story always stays with me.

And I tell it to you because I know that you have similar stories. Stories that are embarrassing, stories that don't put you in a good light, stories that illustrate with brightly colored markers who you used to be and how you used to think. I tell you my stories so that you are inspired, motivated, and empowered to tell your stories. Which will inspire and motivate and empower others to tell their stories. If there's one key takeaway I want you to get from this book, it's that antiracism work is about recognizing the humanity in every single person. When I look back at my life, I see very clearly that my failure to recognize the humanity in every single person is my biggest contribution to perpetuating racism. When I haven't bothered to learn about or listen to their story, when I have chosen judgment instead of empathy, indifference instead of compassion, certainty over curiosity—those are the missed opportunities to elevate humanity.

Sharing our stories is frightening as hell. Sharing our stories is vulnerable, raw, and unpredictable. Sharing our stories never gets easy. It's challenging every single time. I've been sharing my stories for twenty years, and it's still scary. But I do it anyway. Because I know the world needs it. I know that when I share my stories I bestow my own humanity on others. When I am authentic and courageous, I make the world a slightly better place. A slightly more inclusive place. A slightly less racist place. A slightly more human place.

And if there's one thing the world needs more of, it's humanity. Please consider contributing your humanity to the world. Tell your stories.

Stories Matter

Stories matter.

Your story matters. My story matters. Our stories matter. The stories we tell matter. The stories we don't tell matter.

Stories about race and racism and injustice and discrimination matter.

Stories about gender inequity and gender pay gaps and sexual assault and imposter syndrome and old boys' networks and bro culture matter.

Stories about people who are transgender and gender nonconforming and gender non-binary matter.

Stories about people who are gay and lesbian and bisexual and intersex and queer matter.

Stories about leadership and allyship and being an accomplice and a co-conspirator matter.

Stories of privilege and power and social capital and social justice and equity and diversity and inclusion and belonging matter.

Stories of empathy and vulnerability and compassion and connection and trust and relationships and humanity matter.

Stories of mindfulness and self-awareness and fear and courage and shame matter.

Political stories and professional stories and personal stories and local stories and international stories matter.

Sad stories and happy stories and painful stories and uncomfortable stories and hopeful stories matter.

You matter. I matter. Our stories matter.

Your Truth Will Set Us Free

A few years ago I went to a storytelling workshop put on by my friends Julian Mocine-McQueen and Heather Box, founders of The Million Person Project.

So many good takeaways from that night—and their work in general.

One overarching message that has stuck with me is this:

Your truth will set us free.

Your truth.

Will set *us* free.

The idea that sharing personal stories and being publicly vulnerable is decidedly not egotistic or narcissistic.

In fact, just the opposite is true. Not telling your story is an act of selfishness.

By not telling your story you're depriving others of the inspiration they may need to step into their full selves.

Telling your personal story is one of the best ways to show inclusive leadership. To shape cultures of belonging. To build relationships and trust and connection. To be antiracist.

I am very open with my story and how it has shaped me into the person I am today. This is very intentional and strategic.

My truth may set *you* free. And you. And you. And who knows who else?

That's the world I want to live in. A world where people feel safe to share their truth without fear of rebuke or social isolation.

And I need you to help me create that world. Share your truth. You may just set someone free.

Remove the Shame

"If we can share our story with someone who responds with empathy and understanding, shame can't survive."

– Brené Brown

This passage encapsulates why I center strategic storytelling in my antiracism and social justice work.

We don't tell enough stories, especially in a workplace setting.

We focus on business and results and efficiency and productivity and innovation and deadlines and deliverables and revenue and client acquisition and customer service...

But do we really know each other? Do we really trust each other? Are we really connected?

Do we really appreciate, value, and embrace our own and each other's unique lived experiences that have shaped our perspectives and how we navigate the world?

I don't believe we do.

We're afraid to be vulnerable. We're afraid of exposing our true selves because it's too revealing, too raw, too emotional, too damn scary.

What if people judge me? Don't like me? Laugh at me? Hurt me? Demote me? Fire me?

Senior leaders especially need to share their stories. Set the tone. Model public vulnerability. Explicitly give permission for a storytelling culture.

Remove the stigma of bringing your true self to work. Remove the doubt and uncertainty and discomfort.

Remove the shame.

Let's start telling our stories.

Back Before I Started
Telling My Stories

"Can we trust each other with our true stories?
That's where we find belonging."

– Jennifer Brown

Back when I was too embarrassed to tell anyone I had a gay dad.

Back when my family was too poor to afford cool clothes and I got bullied.

Back when I had a "job" stealing quarters out of newspaper racks because it paid more than minimum wage at Souplantation.

Back when I was ashamed to live in an apartment when most of my friends lived in houses.

Back when I was casually racist and sexist and homophobic—not out of malice, but out of ignorance.

Back when I judged people on whether they were good at sports.

Back when I chose my friends by the amount of beers they could shotgun.

Back when I almost flunked out of college because of aforementioned drinking and sports.

Back when I didn't read.

Back when I listened to A Tribe Called Quest and thought I had "culture."

Back when I mocked and dismissed and othered and ignored everything I didn't know or care about.

Back when I wasn't truly connected to anything, or anyone, or anywhere.

Back when I was lying and covering and bullshitting.

Back when I was insecure and lonely and immature.

Back when I didn't know to whom or where or what I belonged.

Back when I was afraid to trust.

Back before I started telling my stories.

Reflecting On the Old You

Sharing stories of your evolution of consciousness is a much more authentic and compelling way to show your support and commitment to a more antiracist, socially just, and equitable world than merely stating that you support and are committed to a more antiracist, socially just, and equitable world.

The latter might seem more powerful, more concise, more relevant, more committed. But without any personal backstory or context, these statements alone often come across as trite platitudes or insincere boilerplates that we've heard from a thousand other people.

We want to know how you've changed. How you've arrived at your present stance and world view.

We want to know what you used to think and do (or not think and not do), and what and why and how you learned to evolve your thinking.

Then, when we hear your current position, it's more believable.

When you're vulnerable sharing your past thinking, your mistakes, your embarrassing history, we are more likely to connect with you on a deeper level. We're more likely to trust that your current position is honest.

It's not always easy to explore and reflect upon the old you who was unaware of everything that the new you believes so strongly.

And, when you invest the effort to more accurately and humbly articulate your journey, you will make a greater impact.

Keep Doing Your Thing

I'm a junior in college walking down the busiest party street in town on a Friday night.

Most everyone I pass, in their drunken debauchery, laughs and points at me.

"Hey, look at *that* guy! What's he doing? Oh my god, he's got a—harmonica!" Pause. Hilarity. Pause. "And—he's *playing* it!" Side-splitting hilarity.

Astute observation indeed. I was playing a harmonica. Not very well but I was playing it.

I'd been listening to old blues records for three years— including harmonica legends like Sonny Terry, Sonny Boy Williamson, and Little Walter—and I finally decided I'd play harmonica too.

That afternoon, I had bought a harmonica—in the key of B to play the blues of course—and was ambling down the street that night playing decidedly un-bluesy melodies, ignoring the laughing and pointing.

Within a year I was sitting in with local blues bands. A few years later playing in my own band, recording with other people, playing all over town.

Tons of new friends, good times, amazing experiences, wonderful memories. And an instrument that fits in my pocket.

Not sure what was so funny about a guy walking down the street playing a harmonica. I do it all the time. It's just my thing.

And you should do your thing too. Even if people laugh at you.

The Vast Dynamism
of the Human Condition

June 25, 1998. Leave Yuma at midnight. Head north along the Colorado River.

1986 Mazda B2200 pickup with a shell. Carpet kit with a comforter, a bag of clothes, and a guitar.

Two years out of college. Philosophy degree. Deep desire to explore—myself and the country.

Drive for four months. Twenty five thousand miles.

Forty seven states.

The Salmon River in Idaho. Mosquitos the size of woodpeckers in Minnesota. Jazz in the Village. Body surfing in the Outer Banks of Carolina.

Honky-tonking in Nashville. Too much rum on Bourbon Street. Singing with hundreds of new friends at a piano bar in San Antonio. Surreal sunsets in Arches, Utah.

The I-25 freeway where the house where I was born used to be in Albuquerque.

The freedom. The curiosity. The growth. The experience. The learning. The people. The equanimity. The beauty. The stories. The belonging.

The vast dynamism of the human condition.

Now, a mortgage, two cars, two kids, property taxes, a career, responsibility, sore joints, thinning hair, financial security, infinite wisdom and maturity.

All the mod cons. All the middle class trappings.

And the same spirit. The same approach. Friendships. Relationships. Self-actualization. Focus. Freedom from choice. Empathy. Curiosity. Belonging.

The vast dynamism of the human condition. Still.

Now from my basement.

We Are More Than Our Work

Monday, January 26, 2009. 12:30pm. Oakland.

I walk into my sixth-grade classroom for my afternoon lessons. My phone rings. It's my wife.

"Emergency C-section. Tonight. 6:30."

I find a substitute, and rush to San Francisco to my wife's aunt's house, across the park from where my twins will be born in a few hours.

I eat a turkey sandwich. I am calm.

In a nervous, excited, scared, happy kind of way.

We drive through Golden Gate Park to the hospital. I sign a bunch of papers. I wear a hospital gown and a shower cap. I almost shit my pants. I try to blame the turkey sandwich.

At 6:41pm my son is born. 6:42 my daughter.

I'm a father. I'm crying tears of joy. My kids are screaming tears of life.

Now they are twelve. I'm still happy.

We are more than our work. We all have intrinsic motivations. We all have a "why."

Each why is unique, personal, and important. Mine. Yours. Everyone's.

Are we working in spaces that allow us to share our "why"? That allow us to be vulnerable? To be our dynamic, beautiful selves?

Or do we feel the need to cover? Trapped behind a mask in a cage of professionalism.

When we share personal stories, we give others permission to share theirs. We build trust and connection.

We create inclusive communities and cultures where everyone feels like they belong.

Feeling Good to Be Alive

I miss the commute. Being alone with hundreds of people.

The walk from the BART parking garage to the BART platform. Passing shuttle buses, cop cars, bicyclists, panhandlers, musicians.

Lines of people weaving around the two platforms. Waiting for trains to arrive. Four tracks with trains in four directions.

People reading papers, books, phones, and each other. Old. Young. Black. White. Asian. Latino. In wheelchairs. With bikes. Professional. Casual. Hip. Nerdy. Barefoot.

Cars whizzing by on the freeway—light traffic going east, heavy traffic going west.

Slithering into a crowded car. Backpack between my legs. Book open ready to read. Headphones on. Standing in a sea of humanity. Living.

Breathing in BO, pot, ass, stale breath, breakfast sandwiches, perfume, gum, deodorant—an intermingling cacophony of aromas.

The train lurches forward. Lose balance. Bump into people. Mouth sorry. Regain balance. Resume my book.

Each stop. People getting on. Getting off. Smiles. Frowns. Sighs. Coughs. Conversations. Games. Movies. Phone calls.

Under the bay. Into the city. Emerge in a new world. Tall buildings. Street cars. Mopeds. Scooters. Joggers. Suits. Peddlers.

Walk to an office. Ready to work.

Experiencing the vast dynamism of the human condition.

Feeling good to be alive.

We All Want the Same Things

Even people who appreciate the art of storytelling to create antiracist workplace cultures still see it as a "nice-to-have."

As if storytelling were just a more fun, creative way to influence decision makers and create environments where everyone feels like they belong and can flourish.

But, they say, it doesn't trump data and unconscious bias training and accountability metrics and quotas and telling people that if they don't hire X people from Y backgrounds by Z date, they're not gonna get their bonus.

No. Storytelling is a decidedly strategic approach to both achieve statistical goals and results that look neat and shiny in quarterly reports, and change people's hearts and minds about the vast dynamism of the human condition.

To be candid, most people don't care if there are X people from Y backgrounds in Z departments. Not because they're jerks (although some are), but because they're focusing on other things.

Numbers and charts and data don't motivate and inspire and break down barriers. People's stories do.

When you share your own stories, and help other people share theirs, we realize that we all want the same things.

To be seen and valued for who we are. To be our full selves.

Stories matter. Let's start telling them more often.

Telling Stories Can Change the World

"Stories are unprofessional."

"I'm too high up in the company to tell stories."

"My team doesn't want to hear my stories."

"I don't have any good stories."

"Most stories are boring anyway."

"Why would I tell stories when there's work to do?"

"Business is about profit, not stories."

"I don't know how to tell a story."

"I'm an introvert and don't like to tell stories."

"Why would people trust me more if I told more stories?"

"Telling stories is too vulnerable; they make me look weak."

"Leadership isn't about stories; it's about results."

"The board would fire me if I sat around and told stories."

"This isn't a Moth Story Hour; this is business!"

"Oh, look at the little storyteller... isn't he cute?"

"Isn't everyone's story basically the same?"

"What's all this stuff about stories and visibility and representation?"

"I am here to work; not to listen to stories."

"Telling stories is too revealing."

"What if someone tells me a story and I start to cry."

"Are we really 'hardwired to listen to stories'?"

"Do stories really connect us?"

"If I listen to someone's story, does that mean I have to care more about them?"

"Do stories really create belonging?"

"Do stories really level the playing field?"

"Do you honestly think that telling stories can change the world?"

Section 7: An Invitation to Reflect

1. Do you recognize the humanity in every single person—including yourself? Why or why not?

2. Can you clearly articulate your antiracist narrative—who you used to be, who you are, and who you are becoming? Why or why not?

3. What is challenging about publicly sharing your stories? What are the benefits?

4. How do storytelling and public vulnerability fundamentally change the conversation about race and racism?

5. I use the phrase "the vast dynamism of the human condition" a lot. What does that phrase mean to you? Why is it relevant to confronting racism?

SECTION 8

Confronting Racism with Irreverence and Satire

Jared Karol

Laughing to Keep From Crying

*"Satire is traditionally the weapon of the powerless
against the powerful. I only aim at the powerful.
When satire is aimed at the powerless, it's not
only cruel—it's vulgar."* – Molly Ivins

He was a fourth-grade boy named Jimmy Naumbertu, and it was his turn to be *Boy of the Week.* Immensely popular with all the other boys at Werbet Erthenew Elementary School for Boys, mostly because he treated them like absolute garbage, Jimmy brought in for show-and-tell one of his own turds, a turd that one of his three nannies had fished out of the toilet that morning and put in a plastic container for him to carry to school. His parents would have prepared his presentation for him but his mother was at the golf club drinking morning martinis and smoking cigars, while his father was at their Napa home having an affair with the housekeeper. At the end of the school day, Jimmy showed his turd to all his classmates and asked them to tell him what they smelled. When they couldn't identify any smell, he claimed triumphantly that of course they didn't smell anything because Jimmy Naumbertu's shit doesn't smell, and the entire class of idolatrous boys erupted into thunderous applause. Then, propelled by this momentous fanaticism, they lifted Jimmy Naumbertu onto their shoulders and smashed through the school doors and out into the street chanting "Naum-ber-tu! His-shit-doesn't-smell!" They carried on this way through the city for hours, into the sunset, until all that could be seen was the shape of a man with his fists raised in triumph silhouetted by the sun.

Anyway, that was the synopsis of *Boy of the Week*, the first short story I ever wrote back in 2002. Jimmy Naumbertu, of course, wasn't a real kid, and Werbet Erthenew wasn't a real school, but they combined to create a highly exaggerated amalgamation of absurd traits and mindsets and behavioral patterns and contexts I had observed in real kids and their real parents and their real nannies and their real privilege and their real ignorance and their real arrogance and their real wealth and their real whiteness at a real school. I took a little bit from the White kid who said it was okay for him to break the rules and ride the school elevator by himself because he had one in his house and he knew how to operate it. I took a little bit from the White kid who read aloud a math word problem about someone named Jew-Ann, and when I asked him if he read that right, he said yes, J-U-A-N, Jew-Ann. And I took a little bit from the many, many White kids whose mom picked them up from school in the Mercedes on Mondays, and whose first nanny picked them up in the Porsche SUV on Wednesdays, and whose second nanny picked them up in the Audi on Fridays. And I took a little bit from the mom who at the holiday break and the end of the school year gave every teacher who taught her son a sealed monogrammed envelope with a crisp hundred-dollar bill inside, as if we were the hired help. And I took a little bit from the White moms who could be overheard gossiping about the audacity of the parents of the only three Black kids in the second grade to demand that their sons be in the same class so one of them did not drown in a classroom of whiteness all by himself with no life vest. I took all this information and more, and I created Jimmy Naumbertu, his family, and the Werbet Erthenew school community.

When I was Jimmy's age, my mom would cash her paycheck every Friday and distribute the one and five and ten-dollar bills amongst the slots of the accordion envelope labeled groceries, haircuts, gas money, electric bill, and whatever else we needed to spend our money on to survive. When I was a kid our one car was a Chevy Sprint. When I was a kid, I had no nannies, no vacation homes, and no elevators in our six hundred square foot rented townhouse. When I was a kid, I never saw a hundred-dollar bill, let alone held one in my hand. Compared to mine, Jimmy's world was a bizarre, alternative reality that until then I had never spent much time in. Being so up close and personal in this world daily was a new experience for me, almost surreal, and making fun of it was the only way I could think to process what I was observing. Soon enough I came to understand the rules of this world, but I was unwilling to abide. I wasn't driven by bitterness or resentment or jealousy, and I like to think that I had no malicious intent. But even though I was only a few years into my cultural fluency journey, I was able to clearly recognize how the values and social expectations that the people in this world upheld contributed to society's gross inequities. I knew enough to know that indifference and condescension and a failure to use racial privilege and power and influence as a force for good exacerbated these inequities.

The problem was that I didn't really know what to do about it. I was just entering the bomb-throwing stage of my revolution, and my lack of experience led me to believe that there were no alternatives other than to throw my homemade bombs indiscriminately at any people or ideas or institutions that I considered my enemy. With no awareness or appreciation of subtlety or nuance, I went with the carpet bombing approach, wiping out everything in my path. It was the only way I saw I could assert my agency and autonomy, to use what little power I felt I had to make my voice heard above the cacophonous din. I know now that my approach was all very superficial and desperate, and wholly ineffective. It wasn't that my acerbic tone, my sarcasm, my snark had no place or value; it was just that it was the only approach I used. I had no variety, and any cleverness I may have expressed was severely limited by my caustic attitude. I invited precisely zero people to dialogue, I opened precisely zero doors for discussion, and I created precisely zero opportunities for constructive conversation that may have perhaps led to some change. In my arbitrary bomb-throwing I ended up bombing my house too, trapping myself underneath the many layers of sardonic rubble with no one around, let alone inclined, to help me climb out.

But eventually I climbed out. With maturity, I learned the value of discernment. I learned that irreverence and satire can be effective ways to share a new perspective, to illustrate a point, to challenge people to think differently, to move the needle, to drive impact and affect change. But there has to be some substance behind it. There has to be some wisdom. There has to be some greater motive than straight-up ridicule and mockery. And at the bottom of it all, there has to be humanity. Elevating humanity has to be the driving force. When I created Jimmy Naumbertu, I was not inspired or motivated by humanity, and the only thing I was elevating was my ego. I was defiantly in permanent attack mode, ready and willing to crush with my droll wit all perceived enemies who were unlucky enough to cross my warpath. I had no larger purpose or stated goal. I made a few people laugh, and more than a few people cringed.

I recently reread *Boy of the Week* and the three or four other pieces I wrote back then in the same vein. I did laugh a bit, transporting myself back in time to those formative years of my personal development and cultural fluency journeys. But I also cringed at my cruelty and ruthlessness, at my undisguised meanness. And I cringed at my inhumanity. There's nothing funny about racism. It has been the scourge of our existence since European slave traders invented the concept of race several hundred years ago. Racism has, and continues to have, very real consequences for very real people. Namely, all of us. And, as Langston Hughes says, sometimes we have to keep laughing to keep from crying. And as long as that laughter makes us reflect, makes us change, makes us do better, makes us see our own and others' humanity, makes us more clearly recognize the absurdity of racism, and helps us to more regularly confront it with unwavering conviction, then I'm totally fine with laughter.

It's Most Likely Not Too Risky

The general response from many White people when challenged to take action to stop the microaggressions, bullying, discrimination, and racism their Black colleagues face every day in the workplace?

Too risky.

"I'd say something but I'd get fired."

"I can't challenge my boss."

Or my favorite:

"When my boss makes a racist comment in a meeting, I can't stand up, walk across the table, jump down, yell in his face that he's a racist motherfucker, knee him in the nuts, break his nose with my fist while he's doubled over, take off his glasses and chew them into tiny shards, spit the bloody slivers back in his face, toss him over my back in a firefighter's carry, hurl him through the window, and watch him splatter on the streets twenty-seven floors below."

Okay, I paraphrased that one!

And no, in most cases, you can't do that.

The point is, as a White person, your whiteness automatically puts you in a privileged, powerful, influential position.

There are a myriad of impactful ways you can challenge other White people.

Ways that will not get you in trouble. Will not get you fired.

That will make a huge difference to your Black colleagues. That will change the workplace culture for the better.

You just have to be more subtle, more creative, more courageous.

And do it.

I'm Just Not Ready

"I'm not ready to be antiracist. I'm just not there yet."
– Too many White people

The details:

I'm just not ready to give up my privilege.

I'm just not ready to amplify marginalized voices.

I'm just not ready to have conversations that make me feel uncomfortable.

I'm just not ready to read books, listen to podcasts, and watch films centering the experiences of people of color.

I'm just not ready to be self-reflective.

I'm just not ready to challenge the status quo.

I'm just not ready to disrupt the White solidarity I've built up my whole life.

I'm just not ready to stop perpetuating White supremacy.

I'm just not ready to validate the lived experiences of people who are different from me.

I'm just not ready to listen to the stories of people not like me.

I'm just not ready to be humble, empathetic, and compassionate.

I'm just not ready to give up my power.

I'm just not ready to affect change with my social capital, positional authority, and political influence.

I'm just not ready to live in an equitable world.

I'm just not ready to develop my cultural fluency.

I'm just not ready to see people of color as fully human.

I'm just not ready to learn and grow and change.

I'm just not ready to do better.

Check back later though, and maybe I'll be ready.

We Like You, Rhonda,
But You're Just Not a Kappa

A lot of White folks think racism only comes in the "burning cross" variety.

Obvious. Hateful. Aggressive. Murderous.

Easy to identify, condemn, and unite against.

But actually, most racism comes in the "sorority" variety.

Not always easy to identify, condemn, or unite against.

Chris Rock defines sorority racism like this:

"We like you, Rhonda. But you're just not a Kappa."

Kind. Polite. Courteous. Friendly. Smiley.

And racist.

We like you, Rhonda, but you're just not leadership material.

We like you, Rhonda, but you're just not a culture fit.

We like you, Rhonda, but we think Jim should make the presentation.

We like you, Rhonda, but our lunch table is full.

We like you, Rhonda, but you didn't get the promotion.

Sorority racists equate being nice with not being racist.

Sorority racism is difficult for people who don't have racial fluency to recognize it as racism.

Sorority racism is easy to participate in. And just as easy to explain away.

Sorority racism is gender nonspecific.

Sorority racism preserves White supremacy.

Sorority racism thrives in professional, political, and social contexts because people don't realize—or don't care—that they are perpetuating sorority racism.

I think we should file a class action lawsuit against the Greek authorities.

You're Not Racist Because
You Told Me You're Not Racist

That's right, you're not racist because you told me you're not racist. I suppose there's nothing more to be said on the subject.

Since you've told me you're not racist I shouldn't bring up any of your other racist thoughts, actions, or behaviors.

Since you're not racist I shouldn't ask why you laughed at that racist joke at the party last night.

And how could you be racist when you voted for Obama? Twice!

And would a racist like you date a Black woman in college? Unlikely.

And if there was a racist bone in your body you wouldn't be listening to Beyonce on repeat on Spotify.

You can't be racist because you've checked and your ancestors didn't own slaves.

And how on earth can you be racist when you liked two Black Lives Matter posts on social media last week?

And even if you're not racist, you just think Black people would get more support if they stopped talking about race so much.

And you're the least racist person I know, which should be obvious because you live in Brooklyn. Or was it Oakland? Atlanta?

I guess you've made your point. You've repeatedly told me you're not racist. And you're getting pissed because I keep bringing it up.

It's people like me who are racist because we can't stop talking about racism.

You're wondering if I'll ever shut up.

The Rules of the Game

First game of a double header. Black man at the plate. Full count, bottom of the ninth, bases empty with two outs, down by one run.

Team depending on him.

Pitcher winds up. Fastball down the middle. Smacks it to the gap in right center.

Rounds first base. Heading to second. Decides to stretch it to a triple. Sprinting. Hoping to beat the throw.

Dives head first. Creates a cloud of dust.

Risky move to go for a triple. Safe, and his team has a chance. Out, and the game is over.

Waiting to hear the umpire's call. Safe or out?

But all he hears is a crying baby. The dust settles and he sees doctors and nurses and a White woman in a hospital bed holding a newborn baby boy screaming his first breaths.

WTF?

The mom beaming at her son: "Congratulations, Jimmy. You hit a triple. In your first minute of life, you hit a triple."

The crowd cheers.

The Black man is physically blocked from reaching third base. Tagged out. His team loses the game.

The Black man sulks off to the losing dugout. The White mom continues to praise her White son.

"You hit a triple! You hit a triple! You're so talented. Such strong genes. I knew you could do it. I'm so proud of you."

The White baby stays on third base to start the second game.

The crowd continues to cheer wildly.

Only Mean, Ignorant,
Bad People Are Racist

"I was taught the popular folktale of racism: that ignorant and hateful people had produced racist ideas, and that these racist people had instituted racist policies." – Ibram Kendi

I was taught that too. Only mean, ignorant, bad people are racist.

If they'd just stop being mean and bad then racism would end.

But that's not how it works. That lets all of us off the hook who don't think we're "bad" or "mean."

Which is pretty much all of us.

How it really happens, Kendi says, is like this:

Racial discrimination –> racist ideas –> ignorance/hate.

Racially discriminatory policies arise from economic, political, and cultural self-interest. Not hate.

Slavery was economically beneficial to White people so they enslaved Black people.

Then came the racist ideas that Black people were natural slaves, enjoyed slavery, and wouldn't know what to do if they were freed.

When Black people fought those beliefs, White people hated them for being uppity.

The same pattern happens today in organizations.

White people benefit from staying in power, so they hire, promote, reward, and protect other White people.

They'd hire, promote, reward, and protect Black people but they couldn't lower the bar.

Black people say that's effed up. White people hate them for being rude.

Ad infinitum...

No Like. Garbage.

My twins were twenty months old. Dinner at the pop-up folding table in the kitchen. Food everywhere—on faces, fingers, bibs, the table, the floor, me.

Everywhere but on the plate or in the stomach.

I offered my daughter something new. She put it in her mouth. Screwed up her face in disgust. Reached into her mouth. Pulled out the food. Threw it on the floor in a rage. Looked me in the eye. Said:

"No like. Garbage!"

The conviction. The confidence. The courage to challenge authority.

I think she was on to something.

Boilerplate corporate statements in support of Black Lives Matter?

No like. Garbage.

All-White executive teams?

No like. Garbage.

White people saying "all lives matter"?

No like. Garbage.

All White boards?

No like. Garbage.

White people calling the cops on people of color in Central Park and Pacific Heights?

No like. Garbage.

White privilege?

No like. Garbage.

...continued

White cops killing innocent Black people?

No like. Garbage.

White silence?

No like. Garbage.

White fragility?

No like. Garbage.

White tears?

No like. Garbage.

White supremacy?

No like. Garbage.

White people in positions of power using their power to affect change?

Like. Not garbage.

White people throwing their food in a rage at White people who don't seem to get it?

Like. Not garbage.

Don't Make Me Say or
Do Something Racist

I'm not racist, but I'm going to sign this executive order that says it's racist to say that people who are racist are racist.

I'm not racist, but I'm going to invalidate your lived experience as a Black person, because I've had a different lived experience as a White person.

I'm not racist, but why'd you get so upset just because I assumed you got into college on an athletic scholarship?

I'm not racist, but wow, you are *so* articulate.

I'm not racist, but talking about systemic racism is just too divisive.

I'm not racist, but I just don't think you'd be a good fit for the role.

I'm not racist, but why do Oprah and LeBron and other wealthy Black people keep talking about racism?

I'm not racist, but you're really starting to make me feel uncomfortable with all this talk about racism.

I'm not racist, but if Black people just tried harder they would be better off.

I'm not racist, but I've never heard of this redlining thing you keep talking about.

I'm not racist, but how could we live in a racist society when we had a Black president?

I'm not racist, but we're going to remove you from our platform for your antiracist views, but keep the racist people who regularly spout racist views.

I'm not racist, but if you keep talking about racism, you just might make me say or do something racist.

You're Gonna Stop Being Nice

Like most White people, you were taught growing up that racism is bad, Martin Luther King is good, and everything will be okay if you're nice.

This worked as a kid so you figured it would work as an adult and now you live by this simple formula.

You never explored it further. You never bothered to examine if it might be more nuanced, not as simple as that.

Your idea of racism is confined to the "burning cross" kind—lynchings, KKK rallies, angry White people spewing the N-word. Those people are clearly not nice!

You can't understand the more subtle forms of racism—the "fetch me some lemonade" kind. What are people complaining about? Slavery is over. Jim Crow too. We're post-racial. A meritocracy. You have a Black friend.

You dragged your outdated, comfortable worldview with you from childhood. It led to fragility—defensiveness, combativeness, White solidarity—whenever someone brings up systemic racism and privilege.

You lack cultural fluency. You cling to your beliefs. You dismiss out of hand the idea of microaggressions.

Isn't this irrelevant? Shouldn't Black people get over it? Stop bitching? Try harder? Move out of the ghetto? Not be so rude?

It's gotten so bad that if Black people keep grumbling, you're gonna stop being nice.

Not All White People Are Racist

Not all White people are racist. But a lot are.

Not all White dudes are vigilantes hunting and murdering Black joggers. But some are.

Not all White cops use the uniform to protect themselves from their racist actions. But a lot do.

Not all White women work to limit the career opportunities of Black women. But a lot do.

Not all White people use the N word in casual conversations. But a lot do.

Not all White people think Black people should stop playing the race card. But a lot do.

Not all White people dismiss the lived experiences and everyday realities of Black people. But a lot do.

Not all White people believe we live in a meritocracy. But a lot do.

Not all White people refuse to self-reflect and recognize their privilege. But a lot do.

Not all White people tone police when a Black person shares a legitimate concern. But a lot do.

Not all White people consume media from only White voices, lenses, and perspectives. But a lot do.

Not all White people have mostly or solely White social circles and professional networks. But most do.

Not all White people managers, recruiters, and interview panels engage in biased hiring practices against Black people. But a lot do.

Not all White people will react with fragility to this piece. But a lot will.

People Should Really
Drive More Carefully

The nice thing about "not seeing color" is that I move through the world in an insulated, neutral space, totally ignorant of the variety of lived realities experienced by people from different backgrounds than me.

But not seeing color does come with its complications.

For example, the stop light at the busy intersection had a vertical row of gray dots. I didn't know what it meant, so I went through it. Behind me I heard a huge bang. In my mirror I saw a three car pile up. People should really drive more carefully.

That night I went to a basketball game. All ten players were wearing the same grayish uniform. How did they know who to pass to? Was it ten against none? It was really confusing. After the first quarter, I couldn't figure it out, so I left.

The next day I went to the art museum. I'd been told the exhibit was full of vivid depictions of nature that would leave me awestruck. But all I saw was a bunch of gray trees and gray rivers and a big gray ball in the sky. Snoozer! Never going there again.

This is what happens, I guess, when you don't see color. You miss out on a lot of what the world has to offer.

The good news is that all my colleagues are just like me, and I don't have to keep talking about race and identity and underrepresentation all the time.

Scary Books Written by Black People

I shared with my network a book I read: *How To Be Less Stupid About Race*.

It was written by a Black woman, Crystal Fleming.

I was saying how important it is for White people to read books by and about Black people.

I was wondering how many White people went out and bought that book and started reading it.

Probably not many, if any.

Because a lot of White people don't read many books, let alone books written by Black people.

Books by Black people who directly challenge the comfortable world view of White people.

Books that make White people think and self-reflect and grow and explore and self-examine and evolve their consciousness and change their perspective.

White people are afraid to be affiliated with books written by Black people.

Why should I read it? What's in it for me? What will my friends think? You're reading *that* book? The stigma!

Books written by Black people are a threat to the established order of books written by White people.

White people don't feel comfortable engaging in intellectual activity where they are not in control of the narrative. White people feel they have little to learn.

Books written by Black people are scary. Hundreds of blank white pages covered in black ink.

It's much safer to watch reruns of *Leave It to Beaver*.

Thanks for Calling the Tone Police

"Thanks for calling the Tone Police, how can I help you?"

"I'd like to report an incident."

"Yes."

"A Black woman was very rude to me in the break room after I complimented her hair and reached out to touch it."

"Oh my god, that's awful. What did she say?"

"She slapped my hand away, and said something about not being a pet. I don't remember exactly because I was so shocked by her tone."

"I'm so sorry this happened to you. Are you okay?"

"I'm a little shaken, to be honest. You just can't—treat people like that."

"I know. It's becoming an epidemic."

"Do you get a lot of calls like this?"

"Every day! And they're basically the same thing: An overreaction to a perceived injustice."

"Wow! When will people realize that rudeness will not solve their so-called problems?"

"I'm not sure. But that's why the Tone Police are here: to restore civility to the conversation."

"Thank you, Tone Police, for all your work. I feel better just knowing you exist."

"You're welcome. I've logged the incident and will be following up soon with her manager."

"Well, I hope she gets the message. Because things can't go on like this. I mean, how are we supposed to work together in this environment?"

"Rest assured. It will be handled. Thank you for calling the Tone Police. Have a great day."

All Those Times

All those times I was never misgendered.

All those times no one said anything when I walked down the street holding hands with my opposite-sex significant other.

All those times I wasn't followed in a store because of the color of my skin.

All those times when I wasn't afraid for my life when the cops pulled me over.

All those times when I was with people who looked like me in a classroom, at a job, on a team, at an event, in the community, in the neighborhood.

All those times when I got angry and no one accused me of being the angry White guy.

All those times I was assumed to have competence in a domain that I had no experience in.

All those times when the people in the movies and on the TV and in the executive suite and in politics looked like me.

All those times when I easily took the stairs to the second floor when the elevator was out of service.

All those times I offended people and had no idea that I had offended people.

All those times I read books by and about people who looked like me, and lived similar lives to me, and who I could relate to.

All those times I didn't get the extra security check at the airport.

All those times my friends got me the job without an interview.

All those times I got the good table at the restaurant.

All those times...

You Racist Motherfuckers!

You walk into the break room Monday morning to grab a cup of coffee. You overhear your direct supervisor and two of your colleagues, all White men, talking about their weekend golf game.

You mention to them that you golf too and next time you'd love to join the fun.

Your supervisor says he didn't realize you golfed, but they'd definitely invite you if they ever played basketball.

The three of them laugh. You don't.

You are Black. You don't play basketball. In fact, you don't even watch basketball.

You try to decide how to respond.

Do you say, "That's messed up, you racist motherfuckers!" and be accused of being the angry Black man?

Do you say, "You do realize that you are making racist stereotypes based on the color of my skin," and be accused of being too sensitive or playing the race card?

Or do you say nothing—maybe even join in with the laughter—while resentment and bitterness and anger eat away at your heart and soul from the inside, the perpetual microaggressive onslaught devours your spirit and crushes your motivation day after day after day after day...

Before you can respond, the three of them leave the room. You're alone—a Black man with a black coffee in a black humor.

Hell of a way to start the week. Again!

Fade to White

A few reasons why people don't talk about race at work:

I'm uncomfortable.

I don't know what to say.

I'm White so I have nothing to contribute.

I was hired to [insert job function], not talk about race.

Why is it always about race?

Black people always play the race card.

Talking about race is divisive.

Whenever I talk about race, I say the wrong thing.

My manager told us not to talk about race.

My manager has no racial fluency.

My manager is Black and always wants to talk about race.

Politics and work shouldn't mix.

Talking about race is distracting.

What about class and gender?

Our company is a meritocracy.

Slavery happened a long time ago.

My family never owned slaves.

We had a Black president so there's no more racism.

I don't see why race is relevant.

I don't see color.

There's really only one race—the human race.

Race is a social construct, so it doesn't really exist.

...continued

I just want the best person to do the job; I don't care if they're Black, White, purple, or green.

It's easier to talk more generally about "D&I" stuff.

We had an hour-long unconscious bias training already.

I feel guilty because I'm White.

And the film ends with our hero, the status quo, hoisted onto the shoulders of adoring fans and carried off into the sunset.

The screen fades to Bla—uh, I mean, White...

Section 8: An Invitation to Reflect

1. When and how is confronting racism with humor effective? When and how is it not appropriate?

2. What have you heard people say about race and racism that is so absurd you just had to laugh?

3. What do you think Molly Ivins means when she says that satire is the weapon of the powerless against the powerful?

4. If you're White, how does the satirization of White people make you feel? Why do you think you're feeling what you're feeling?

5. What is your immediate thought when you hear someone say, "I'm not racist, but..."?

SECTION 9

Confronting Racism with Leadership

What We Know

*"White people embracing hashtags won't
help us destroy anti-Black racism."*

– Maia Niguel Hoskin, Ph.D.

W e know that on Memorial Day of 2020 a convenience store clerk in Minneapolis, Minnesota called 911 and told police that a Black man had bought cigarettes with a counterfeit twenty-dollar bill. We know that a little over twenty minutes later, that Black man, George Floyd, was dead.

We know what happened to him. He was needlessly murdered. We know an officer kneeled on his neck for nine minutes until he lay there lifeless on the ground. We know he was not the first Black person murdered by the police. We know that for Black people this murder triggered yet again the intergenerational trauma of being Black in White supremacist America. We know what happened in the days and weeks and months following this inhumane murder. We know it sparked outrage, sadness, and protest. We know Black people were angry. We know that other people of color were angry. We know that anyone who identifies as part of any marginalized group is angry.

We know that an increasing number of White people were angry too. We know that an increasing number of White people, perhaps for the first time, saw clearly the outrage and sadness and trauma that their Black colleagues and friends and neighbors experience every day of their lives. We know that many White people tapped into their previously untapped reserves of empathy, compassion, and vulnerability, and were genuinely moved to respond. We know that many White people saw the humanity in Black people. We know that many White people saw their own humanity too. We know that many White people started or joined book clubs and started listening to Code Switch, and started learning about the destruction of Black Wall Street and the murder of Emmett Till and the origins of blackface and the segregationist practice of redlining. We know that many White people realized that they had not previously realized that being Black in America differs from being White in America. We know these realizations led to angst and guilt and shame and embarrassment. We know these realizations inspired many White people to continue on their journey, to accept that they have privilege, to change themselves so they can affect change in their spheres of influence.

We also know that too many White people engaged in superficial acts of performative allyship. We know that too many White people lacked the stamina, courage, and commitment to sustain their efforts beyond the summer of 2020. We know that too many White people's enthusiasm waned when they began to more clearly understand that being antiracist requires ongoing work and commitment. We know that too many of those White people who could not sustain the effort work in corporate spaces. We know that too many of those White people manage other people. We know that too many of those White people are directors and vice presidents and senior executives and chief executive officers. We know that many of those White executives felt compelled or obligated or were told to write antiracist statements and share them publicly. We know that most of those statements were boilerplate trite platitudes that were carefully crafted by comms and PR people. We know that most of those statements lacked subtlety, vulnerability, and conviction. We know that most of those statements were a poor substitute for actually showing up for racial justice, that they were shallow attempts at positioning themselves as caring leaders, that the motivation was to quickly put out a statement to ensure that they were not the only company without a statement. We know that most of those statements were uninspiring and drove no change.

We know that there were also internal statements asking employees to be more empathetic, to be more understanding, to be more curious, to reach out to their Black colleagues, to listen to their Black colleagues, to take the time to get to know their Black colleagues better. We know that very few leaders took the time to follow their own suggestions. We know that very few leaders spent the budget on bringing in trained facilitators who can set up structures to create the space needed to have the conversations that would actually be impactful. We know that very few leaders will take the time to be consistently vocal, to be consistently vulnerable, to consistently show up for their Black colleagues. We know that very few leaders were willing to enter into and stay in uncomfortable conversations, to sit with uncertainty, to be humble, to be coached, to be reverse mentored, to learn and grow and improve.

We know all of this because we've witnessed it. We know all of this because we've experienced it. We know all of this because we've actively taken part in it. We know all of this because we are still witnessing and experiencing and taking part in it. We know we need to do better. We know things will not go back to "normal" and will never go back to normal, that we should not expect or desire or try to fast track a return to so-called normal. We know we need to demand a new normal. We know that in this new normal, we need to hold ourselves and our leaders accountable. We know that in this new normal, leaders with power, influence, and visibility will evolve their consciousness, will elevate their self-awareness, will increase their cultural fluency, will do their personal development work. We know that this work will be difficult for leaders. We know they will mess up and say the wrong things and struggle with how to respond to the criticism that they are engaging in performative allyship. We know that it will be awkward and uncomfortable and clumsy. We know that they don't need to be perfect, but that they need to be genuine, that they need to be part of the solution.

We know that we expect nothing less. We know that we will accept nothing less.

Hey, Those Are My Nipples

In front of the entire school, Tad and Jim, the two biggest kids in seventh grade, lifted me by my nipples and slammed me into the lockers.

There I was, hung up in the shop front window, on display for hundreds of kids to ridicule my nerdy short shorts that John Stockton envied and my scrawny legs that flamingos mocked.

The intention was to humiliate me. And it worked.

I was not scared for my physical safety, but, high up as I was, my already low social capital sunk to deeper depths.

I felt ashamed and embarrassed, filled with a profound resentment and anger that I could not address.

Kids walked by and laughed. Some casually. Some uproariously. No one said or did anything to help me.

I recovered from the incident and moved on with my awkward middle school life. As soon as my mom could afford them, she bought me a pair of longer, more stylish shorts.

I wore them every day for the rest of the year.

We've all, at some point, felt excluded, targeted, or othered for how we look, dress, or speak. For the religion we practice, the food we eat, the people we love, the color of our skin...

These experiences stay with us. They aren't confined to twelve-year-olds in the middle school halls either. Adults in the corporate halls experience them too.

This is why we do the work.

We All Have Different
Lived Experiences

Think of what we lose when we don't intentionally create inclusive cultures of belonging.

The loss of creativity and innovation and productivity and collaboration and...

When people use extra energy to cover part or all of who they are because they don't feel safe bringing their full selves to work.

When managers don't show that they care and that they understand we have interests and needs and lives outside of the office.

When a gay man doesn't come out because he's heard too many homophobic slurs in the break room.

When a single woman downplays her motherhood because she doesn't want people to think she's not dedicated when she leaves early to take her son to soccer practice.

When a Black man doesn't speak up in meetings because there are no other Black people on the team and his White colleagues talk over him.

When a person with invisible disabilities acts as if everything's normal because it's just too hard to explain.

We all have different lived experiences that we bring to work.

If we don't feel our lived experiences are validated and valued, we suppress them.

When we suppress who we are, our mental energy is taken away from our work.

When our mental energy is taken away from our work, our work suffers.

And that hurts us all.

You Cannot Check Out
of the Conversation

Attention White men in senior leadership positions!

There is a big difference between de-centering yourself in the racism and social justice conversation.

And checking out of the conversation altogether.

This difference is crucial.

You are in a position of high visibility. You have major decision-making power. You have authority and prestige and autonomy.

People's careers and psychological safety and sense of belonging are depending on your leadership.

You cannot check out of the conversation.

Marginalization and discrimination and unfair hiring practices and old boys' networks and bro culture and daily microaggressions and systemic inequity and institutionalized racism and compounding privilege and intersectional disadvantages and othering aren't "their" problems.

These realities aren't realities that only apply to "those people."

These are everyone's realities to address. To change. To improve. To evolve.

You cannot check out of the conversation. You have to be present. You have to educate yourself. You have to listen. You have to be humble.

You have to do better.

You have to develop a point of view. You have to speak out. You have to be an ally. An advocate. An accomplice for change.

People are depending on you. You have to step up.

How Do We Break The Cycle?

One of the reasons we don't have workplaces where everyone feels like they belong is because we don't know each other.

Sure, we work on projects, and we eat lunch, and we may even do some social stuff with select colleagues.

But do we share with each other more than the superficial traits about who we are?

Do we feel like we know—really know!—our coworkers?

Do we know their pains and triumphs and dreams and fears?

Or, are we trapped in a realm of static "professionalism" and boring decorum?

Why are we afraid to be vulnerable, to reveal truths about ourselves that show our deeper motivations and inspirations and reasons for living?

It's that lack of vulnerability that makes us inaccessible, closed-off, mysterious.

Every day—every hour!—we miss opportunities to deepen relationships, to deepen connections, to deepen trust.

How do we break this cycle?

Someone has to take the lead. Someone has to give permission to others to be vulnerable by being vulnerable themselves.

Someone has to model the behaviors and mindsets that we need in the workplace.

I try to be that person on a regular basis. Will you be that person with me?

Using Our Social Capital
More Strategically

One of the main obstacles to building inclusive communities is that we assume that our subjective experience is the objective truth.

That our norm is *the* norm.

That our world view is more or less the same as *everyone's* world view.

Armed (and dangerous) with this perspective, we don't bother to explore, understand, or appreciate that what is true for us is not necessarily true for others.

That there are external factors that contribute to inequality. That people on the downside of power may work just as hard as people on the upside and not see the same results.

That privilege is real. That systemic racism and institutionalized sexism and legal homophobia are real.

As long as we choose to stay blind to the lived experiences of people with different backgrounds, we will continue to find it difficult to relate, and we will continue to dismiss the concerns that we have chosen to not understand.

It is our responsibility as people who care about social and racial justice, equity, inclusion, and belonging to disrupt the status quo by educating ourselves.

By familiarizing ourselves with other people's realities. By listening, reading, immersing, and advocating.

This means using our social capital more strategically.

Are you up for the challenge?

The PLU Syndrome
and Dominant Group Fragility

I believe that our workplaces are not as diverse and inclusive as they should be because of two interrelated dynamics:

The PLU (People Like Us) Syndrome and Dominant Group Fragility.

Both manifest in sometimes overt, sometimes discreet, and often discriminatory ways.

The PLU Syndrome works like this:

"No way, you went to Stanford too? You'll love it here. Can you start Monday?"

Or

"Well, we would like to hire more Black engineers, but we don't want to lower the bar."

Or

"I think Jim over there is a little... you know... different."

Dominant Group Fragility is an expansion of Robin DiAngelo's *White Fragility* concept in which a dominant group member becomes defensive, dismissive, or otherwise disengages from a difficult conversation.

It might look like this:

"Are you saying we shouldn't hire people from the top schools?"

Or

"Does the race card need to be played every time a Black person doesn't get the promotion?"

...continued

Or

"What are you saying, that I'm homophobic?"

The PLU Syndrome perpetuates dominant group comfort and stability to seek out (and hire, and promote, and praise) other "people like us."

When raised as problematic, fragility kicks in and prevents productive dialogue about what we should do to change the dynamic.

Redistributing the Emotional Labor

So much of antiracism, social justice, inclusion, equity, and belonging work is about redistributing the emotional labor.

Far too often people from marginalized and underrepresented groups take on most, if not all of the emotional labor of educating others, righting wrongs, correcting inaccuracies, and pointing out offensive language and actions.

For there to be change, people from dominant groups need to step up and take on more of this emotional labor.

Dominant group members need to work to remove that burden.

They need to educate themselves on the lived experience of others. They need to read. And listen. Be humble. And courageous.

They need to get over their fragility and privilege. They need to step out of their comfort zone.

And they need to act.

White people need to relieve the emotional labor of Black people.

Straight people need to relieve the emotional labor of gay people.

Cis people need to relieve the emotional labor of trans people.

Etc.

If you are a member of one or more dominant groups, what are you doing to be a true ally, advocate, or accomplice?

How are you challenging the status quo? Disrupting the norm?

How are you driving impact and affecting change?

Are you doing your part to redistribute the emotional labor?

Leaders Show Vulnerability
in Times of Uncertainty

As a leader, one simple way you can be more inclusive in times of uncertainty is to show vulnerability.

A strategic way to do that is to share personal stories in your communications to your team, company, clients, and customers.

Stories, when told well, build trust and connection.

Stories illuminate our common humanity.

Stories build community across diverse backgrounds because the personal is universal.

The feelings and emotions you're experiencing? I'm experiencing them too.

If I feel like you get me, and genuinely care about my well-being, I'll be a lot more forgiving of your mistakes and flaws.

If you can tap into how we're more similar than different, I will have more confidence in, and commitment to, our shared goals.

When you show public vulnerability, when you reveal who you are, when you are accessible and relatable, when you convince me that you're a real human being with real emotions and doubts and uncertainties and hopes and dreams, then I'm more likely to believe what you say.

If you share what personally inspires and motivates you, I will be more inspired and motivated *by* you.

On the other hand, if you go all robotic and drop corporate jargon filled with trite platitudes, I'm going to think you're a jerk and ignore everything you say.

Your choice.

You Don't See the Irony

You're a people manager, VP, executive, or otherwise in a position of influence and power.

You haven't done your personal development work, so you don't know how to create a culture of inclusion and belonging.

You lack racial fluency, relational agility, and cultural humility. You don't know how to connect with people who have different lived experiences than you.

You navigate the world with outdated and inaccurate story lines:

I have no time for empathy.

EQ is for wusses.

People just make excuses.

It's a meritocracy.

But these are simply your narrow story lines. Your ingrained habits. Your stubborn perspectives you won't let go.

You don't realize that you are the problem. That you are driving attrition. That you are sapping motivation. That you are uninspiring. That you are the cause of low productivity, lack of innovation, less creativity.

When any of this is brought to your attention, you dig in. You rebut. You dismiss. You fuel the devolution with your righteous indignation and fragility.

Dynamics that could easily improve, persist, because you are unwilling to reflect and change. You strengthen the story line at the cost of the "results" you claim to want in the first place.

And of course you don't see the irony.

Educate Yourself and Do Better

It's not the responsibility of Black people to educate White people about "the Black experience."

White people need to educate themselves and do better.

It's not the responsibility of gay people to educate straight people about what it's like to be gay.

Straight people need to educate themselves and do better.

It's not the responsibility of trans people to continually remind cis people of their cis-normative actions and behaviors.

Cis people need to educate themselves and do better.

It's not the responsibility of women to point out to men that their old boys' networks and bro culture are perpetually contributing to the continued scarcity of women in leadership positions.

Men need to educate themselves and do better.

It's not the responsibility of people with visible or invisible disabilities to educate non-disabled people on what it's like to not have access to what you need to succeed at your job.

Non-disabled people need to educate themselves and do better.

People whose dimensions of diversity place them wholly or partly in the dominant group need to take the responsibility of educating themselves about the lived experiences of people who are part of one or more underrepresented groups.

Ease the burden of responsibility and emotional labor.

Educate yourself.

Do better.

People Are Depending On You

One of the main reasons people from the dominant culture (i.e., cis, straight, White men like me) don't get involved in conversations about diversity, race, identity, and other uncomfortable and unfamiliar topics (to them), is because they're afraid that they're going to make a mistake.

They're afraid they don't have the subject matter expertise to contribute. They're afraid that they don't know what they're talking about. They're afraid that they'll be scolded for "doing it wrong."

You have to get over your fear. You have to absorb criticism. You have to be open to learning. You cannot take things personally.

You have to do your personal development and your cultural fluency work on your own time.

And, while you're evolving your consciousness, you have to be an active ally, advocate, and accomplice in creating an inclusive culture where everyone feels like they belong.

This isn't "their" problem. And it's not "your" problem. It's everyone's responsibility to educate themselves, learn from their mistakes, and stay present in the conversations that impact all of us.

You can't wait to "arrive" before you start contributing. No one arrives. We're all here already. Now. Start doing the work.

People are depending on you.

Awaken All of Yourself

*"If you want to awaken all of humanity,
awaken all of yourself."* – Lao Tzu

Leaders, please hear this clearly:

No one can make you do the right thing.

Dozens of laminated, multi-colored, poster-sized lists of do's and don'ts strategically placed in elevators and snack areas and conference rooms do not create an inclusive culture.

No training on unconscious bias or cross-cultural awareness or avoiding stereotypes or harassment or empathy or mindfulness or microaggressions or anything else will lead to a fundamental change in company culture.

A thousand ERGs, diverse interview and candidate slates, women's leadership initiatives, Pride days, solidarity marches, and cultural celebrations will not move the needle.

If you don't intentionally commit to elevating your self-awareness and cultural fluency.

Nothing will change if you don't read and listen and learn and get coaching and grow and expand and check your biases and be humble and be vulnerable and admit mistakes and publicly advocate for people "not like you" and use your influence to change policy and actively participate in uncomfortable conversations.

If you're not willing to do all of that, then it's just a big facade. A performance. And nothing will change.

So, are you ready to do the work?

Be Courageous Until You
No Longer Need to Be

People tell me I'm courageous for speaking up about the injustices that impact people on the downside of power.

That it's courageous for a White guy to amplify the voices of people of color.

And risk my social capital with other White people.

That it's courageous for a cis, straight guy to amplify the voices of members of the LGBTQ community.

And risk my privileged gender normative status.

That it's courageous to speak up on behalf of women who are marginalized.

And alienate my bros.

I suppose there's some merit to the praise. I humbly receive it, and it is part of what motivates me to keep speaking up.

And, it doesn't really feel that courageous anymore.

It just feels like—what I do.

When I didn't have confidence in my beliefs and values and principles. When I hadn't developed my cultural fluency. When I was just a wee bud on the flower of self-actualization.

That's when it felt more courageous. When it felt more like a risk.

It took more courage then because I didn't realize that I didn't care about what I might lose.

So, as you travel on your journey: Be courageous. Share your power. Risk your social capital. Risk your privilege.

Until it's no longer courageous. Until it's no longer a risk.

Because you don't care about what you might lose.

Dumping Oil on a
Flaming Pyre of Biases

If you know me, and peruse my posts on LinkedIn, you know I'm an avid reader.

Furthermore, you know I believe that reading books written by and about people "not like you" is the best way to elevate your cultural fluency.

I believe that a lack of cultural fluency stems from a lack of curiosity, a lack of empathy, and a lack of connection to people you perceive to be different.

And of course you know that marginalizing, suppressing, or patronizing people you perceive to be different is the quickest and best way to maintain the perpetuity of the status quo, bro culture, and old boys' networks—to continue the normalization of dominant narratives.

And you no doubt also know that when dominant narratives are desperately clung to, the clinging hands are holding a barrel of oil and dumping it on the already flaming pyre of biases (conscious and unconscious), microaggressions, discrimination, and other majority-group-accepted everyday prejudices.

And I'm here to tell you—because you may not realize it—that your choice to not read books at all or to only read books by and about people like you is fueling the fire of racial, social, political, legal, and professional inequities all around us.

Why don't you help put the fire out?

Read.

Why Would You Do That?

Would you tell a contractor to build your house out of balsa wood? Probably not.

Would you tell a vintner to make your wine with horse piss instead of grapes? Probably not.

Would you tell a professional athlete to prepare for games by chugging beers? Probably not.

Would you tell a tailor to make your suit out of fiberglass? Probably not.

Would you tell a sushi chef to give you three-day-old salmon? Probably not.

Would you tell a lawyer to just wing the defense argument in your murder trial? Probably not.

You know why you would never do any of that?

Because even if you're not a contractor, vintner, athlete, tailor, sushi chef, or lawyer, you know enough to know those suggestions are absurd.

So why if you're cisgender do you have no problem telling transgender people they're confused?

And why, if you're White, do you have no problem gaslighting Black people?

And why, if you're a man, are you so comfortable mansplaining things to women?

Why do you use your privilege, power, and social capital to speak with such disparaging authority on the lived experiences of people you know little to nothing about?

What weird combination of hubris and malice has led you to dismiss with such confident disdain another person's truth?

And, most importantly, when are you going to change?

Imagine What Our World Would Be

Imagine if the most influential, most powerful, most visible leaders were willing to be vulnerable.

Imagine if they saw vulnerability not as a weakness, but as a show of strength.

Imagine if they revealed a little bit of who they were behind the veneer of "successful, competent, all-knowing business person."

Imagine if they humanized themselves by admitting mistakes, by being transparent, by sharing what they didn't know, by asking for support.

Imagine if the people who worked for these leaders saw them as real live human beings with feelings and emotions, hardships, doubts, uncertainties, and challenges.

Imagine if they modeled empathy and compassion and curiosity and equanimity.

Imagine if they consistently and intentionally strove to create a culture of belonging for themselves and everyone in their sphere of influence.

Imagine if we could relate to them, and trust them, and respect them as human beings.

Imagine if we were able to truly connect with them.

Imagine if we actually had a meaningful, non-hierarchical relationship with them.

Imagine if we felt we could be vulnerable with them, admit to them our struggles, doubts, fears, and worries.

Imagine what our companies would be?

Imagine what our world would be?

Uplifting Underrepresented Voices Amplifies All Voices

I am not an expert in antiracism and social justice work.

I am not a thought leader. Or an authority. Or a specialist.

I have not "arrived" anywhere. I have not crossed a finish line. I am not enlightened.

What I have done for the past twenty years is continually elevate my self-awareness while also elevating my awareness of the lived experiences and realities of people "not like me."

Sure, I know all the industry words and phrases and jargon, but that's not the work.

The work is not sexy. Or showy. Or meant to impress anyone. This work is about driving impact and affecting change.

I do the work because I care about people. Because I'm curious. Because I'm grounded. Because I know that building relationships changes the world. Because uplifting underrepresented voices amplifies all voices.

I suspect that some people doing so-called "culture" work have come to the conclusion that they have "arrived" and that there is no more to learn.

There is no finish line. Like me, you will likely never be an expert or an authority.

If you choose to do your personal development and cultural fluency work, what you will become is an empathetic champion of your self-actualization.

Which puts you in a good position to champion the needs of others.

Too Insecure to Be Human

Have you noticed how many senior so-called leaders use command and control tactics to mask underlying insecurity?

Because it's easier to tell people what to do, berate them if they don't do it like you want, and then question their skills, commitment, loyalty, motivation, and ability, than it is to show a little vulnerability and be a real person.

That inability and unwillingness of so-called senior leaders to allow others to see their humanity creates a culture where no one allows anyone else to see their humanity.

So we're left with a stodgy, bureaucratic, hierarchical, fearful, "professional" environment that no one gives two shits about—a workplace culture devoid of humanity.

But filled with small talk and niceties and interpersonal facades and superficial relationships that we conflate with humanity.

And devoid of genuine connection and trust and compassion and genuinely caring about our co-workers.

But because so many so-called senior leaders don't and can't and won't see this, they don't and can't and won't understand why people do mediocre work.

They persist with the tired, uninspiring, superficial, ineffective command and control approach—never once considering that they are the problem.

Repeat. Ad infinitum.

All because they're too insecure to be human.

Section 9: An Invitation to Reflect

1. Why do you think so few leaders take so little substantive, meaningful action toward confronting racism?

2. What roles do courage and vulnerability play in confronting racism? How are they intertwined?

3. If you're in an official leadership position in your organization or community, what specifically are you doing to confront racism?

4. If you're not in an official leadership position, how are you confronting racism by being a change agent?

5. What does a true antiracist, equitable, just workplace culture look like to you? How are you going about making that workplace culture a reality?

SECTION 10

Confronting Racism by Calling People Out

And the Band Plays On

*"Your entire frame of reference will have to change,
and you will be forced to surrender many things
that you now scarcely know you have."*

– James Baldwin

Ray Cyst is your neighbor. He's also your friend, co-worker, boss, and uncle. He's your grocery store clerk, garbage man, barista, and doctor. Your mayor, mechanic, and television game show host. He's the steward on your last flight, your favorite actor, and your kid's friend's dad. He's the bartender at your local pub, the executive at your company, and the guy on your rec soccer team. He's the police officer in your neighborhood and the judge downtown at City Hall.

Ray is about fifty or nineteen or seventy-three. He lives in California or Florida or Delaware or Michigan or Louisiana or Montana or New York. He's kind of reclusive or he's the life of the party always yacking and carrying on. He is interested in politics or engineering or sports or coin collecting. He's wealthy or dirt poor or struggling to pay his bills or has been recently laid off.

Ray Cyst is White. All his friends and social circles are White. He totally identifies as being White or he never thinks about his whiteness. He might be an open and unapologetic White Supremacist or he might not. He might be a Proud Boy or he might not. He might hang out in White Pride Internet chat rooms or he might not. He might read White Supremacist websites and books and propaganda or he might not. He might be aware of systemic racism or he might not. He might deny that we live in a White supremacist world or he might not.

Ray might consciously seek the camaraderie of other White people or he might do it subconsciously. He might admit that he feels safer and more comfortable in the presence of other White people or he might dismiss the idea. He might have an occasional Black friend or acquaintance or he might not. He might be conservative or liberal or independent or apolitical.

One thing Ray does not do is actively support the uplifting of Black people and other people of color. This is because of White solidarity, the often unspoken agreement that White people have with other White people to not destabilize the established racial order that firmly places White people on top, the knee-jerk reaction to defend whiteness not based on the details of any context but based on the coincidence of having a similar skin tone. White solidarity is alluring to Ray because of the comfort of being affiliated with the winners, and the discomfort, uncertainty, and reluctance of being associated with the losers, the unpredictability of how advocating for, aligning with, or defending a Black person, group, or cause may negatively impact the social capital and privilege attained with whiteness.

Ray's White solidarity is rooted in a lack of curiosity—and therefore fluency—in cultural, social, professional, and political issues that shape the lived experiences of Black people and other people of color. He fails to understand and appreciate the sometimes nuanced, sometimes blatant ways that Black people and other people of color are systematically marginalized by institutions, policies, and laws designed to uphold White supremacy. White solidarity is seductive, irresistible to White people like Ray, who have chosen to dismiss what they have been taught as if it doesn't exist.

Ray has millions of brothers and sisters and offspring; millions of uncles, aunts, and cousins; millions of grandparents, grandchildren, and great grandchildren. He clones himself at will, showing up murderously at churches in Charleston, South Carolina, Walmarts in El Paso, Texas, massage parlors in Atlanta, Georgia, BART platforms in Oakland, California, insurrections in Washington D.C. He responds to 911 calls in Minneapolis, Minnesota, attacks and beats and kills elderly Asian people in New York and San Francisco. He is also a regular at baby showers, company potlucks, trivia nights, and children's birthday parties.

Ray and his clones go through life mostly unchallenged, protected and empowered by White solidarity and White Supremacy, swimming blindly in a global petri dish of unexplored, unexamined, and unevaluated views that perpetuate and uphold the White supremacist systems that benefit them. Ray is perpetually emboldened because very few White people have the courage or conviction to call Ray and his clones out on their racism. They are too scared or too nice or too timid or too privileged to risk betraying the interlocking bonds of White solidarity and White supremacy that hold them tight in a womb of safe superiority. Instead, they opt for the comfortable serenity of White solidarity and White supremacy, while ignoring the dehumanization of Black people and other people of color.

Ray Cyst is also an accomplished musician. He is the leader of an all-White band that jams all night every night, never getting tired, a seemingly inexhaustible repertoire of tunes in their music book. Ray's band plays music we're all familiar with, music we've been listening to for centuries, music so ubiquitous we fail to recognize that it's not any good. Ray's music has gone stale. The band has not kept up with the times. Their records are scratched and they play the same notes repeatedly. When we pay closer attention to Ray's band we hear they are out of key, not as tight as we imagined, not as inventive and creative and prolific as we once thought.

It's time for Ray Cyst and his bandmates to retire. But they won't retire voluntarily. The money and prestige are too seductive, the limelight and fame too irresistible. We must demand a new band. A band that plays music we all can enjoy.

A band that plays music for everyone.

Stubbornly Clinging to the Belief
That We Live in a Meritocracy

White people who believe we live in a meritocracy are unable and unwilling to understand or appreciate—let alone embrace or support—the urgency of racial justice.

White people who believe we live in a meritocracy don't and won't understand what "all the fuss is about."

White people who believe the principles of meritocracy extend to everyone, regardless of race, believe they are standing on an unshakeable meritocratic foundation that is inherently fair and equal.

White people who believe we live in a meritocracy unselfconsciously assert that "all lives matter" with defiance and arrogance.

White people who believe we live in a meritocracy believe that because they've worked hard, had misfortunes, been excluded—experienced any number of difficulties that all humans have experienced—that there is nothing racially motivated or racially unjust or racially inequitable about what Black people experience daily.

White people who are unwilling to entertain the idea that we don't live in a meritocracy will continually resist, oppose, and counter any and all efforts that would lead to a meritocracy.

White people who believe we live in a meritocracy rely on unmeritocratic racial privilege to stubbornly cling to the belief that we live in a meritocracy.

When You Say These Things You Look Silly and Racist

Hey White folks, I have a message for you:

We are not targets of systemic racism.

We are not victims because of our race. We are not oppressed because of our race. We are not marginalized because of our race.

I invite you to stop saying your blatant racism is a call for equality. You're embarrassing yourself.

You look silly—and racist—when you say silly and racist things.

For example:

When you say a supermarket ad featuring an all-Black family is racist.

When you say your manager is "over-rotating" because three of the last five people she hired were Black.

When you say Black people would not get murdered if they complied with police.

When you say all lives matter.

When you say diversity is okay as long as we don't lower the bar.

When you say we live in a meritocracy while ignoring the abysmal number of Black folks in leadership positions.

When you say these things you look silly and racist.

And these are just a few examples that come to mind off the top of my head. I could list hundreds more.

Black people having greater access to professional opportunities, gaining more visibility in the media, or talking about the racism they've experienced is not racism.

It's called equity. Even if you feel threatened.

What *is* racism: Defending the status quo of whiteness, and dismissing people who talk about race as racists.

How to Be Racist

"We know how to be racist. We know how to pretend to be not racist. Now let's know how to be antiracist." – Ibram Kendi

How to be racist:

Join a White Supremacist group.

Call the cops on people of color for doing nothing wrong.

Refer to the coronavirus as the "Chinese virus" or "Kung Flu."

Kneel on a Black man's neck for nine minutes.

Shoot a Black man with a shotgun because he was running down the road.

Put the resume with the "Black sounding name" in the "no" pile.

Don't sell the house to the Hispanic family in the upscale neighborhood.

Make jokes about people of color with your White friends.

Harass Black people on social media.

Say "all lives matter" anytime you hear, read, or see "Black Lives Matter."

How to pretend to be not racist:

Tell people you're not racist.

How to be antiracist:

Actively and consistently oppose all racist action, behavior, speech, and policy.

Actively and consistently oppose using your money, votes, influence, and social capital, any politician, initiative, behavior, company, policy, or law that is racist.

Actively and consistently support using your money, vote, influence, and social capital, any politician, initiative, behavior, company, policy, or law that is antiracist.

And, more than anything, stop saying, "I'm not racist."

The Battle Between
the Souls of America

"We the people of the United States do not have a single national soul, but rather two souls, warring with each other. The battle for the soul of America is actually the battle between the souls of America." – Ibram Kendi

One of the main reasons racism persists is because so many people think racism no longer exists.

And of course, it's the most racist people—overtly or covertly—who perpetuate the myth that racism no longer exists.

Who say things "are better than they used to be" and that we have made irrefutable racial progress and that there is no need to talk so often and so seriously about racism...

...while ignoring the fact that every political, social, economic, and cultural advancement toward racial progress is always—*always!*—followed by an aggressive, intentional, angry, resentful response to slow that racial progress.

Slavery ended. The Black Laws and the KKK and Jim Crow and lynching and the burning of Black Wall Street replaced them.

Civil Rights gained momentum.

Dogs and fire hoses and assassinations and disenfranchisement and redlining and mass incarceration and arcane drug laws and "law and order" slowed that momentum.

A Black man became president. We know what happened next...

We do indeed have two souls in this country. Which one is yours?

One of These Kids
Is Not Like the Others

You like coffee. I like tea.

You enjoy folk. I enjoy reggae.

You prefer knitting. I prefer reading.

You say and do and think racist things. I say and do and think antiracist things.

Remember "One of These Kids Is Not Like the Others" from Sesame Street?

Four quadrants with a kid in each one. Three kids doing something similar—kicking a soccer ball, wearing a coat, eating a banana—and the fourth kid doing something different.

It was a good lesson for three-year-olds to identify similarities, recognize differences, and group things by category.

All adults—Sesame Street veterans or not—should be able to do the same.

So why are so many adults unable to see that their racist views are not just a "preference" or a "different opinion" or an "alternative point of view" or "another side of the argument"?

Racism isn't a preference. Racism is racism. And either you say and do and think racist things. Or you say and do and think antiracist things.

It's a choice. Every. Single. Time.

The good news is that one of the most antiracist things you can say or do or think is to admit when you've said or done or thought something racist.

And then stop saying or doing or thinking that thing.

I'm cool with us liking different beverages, enjoying different music, or having different hobbies.

I'm not cool with you being racist.

This Happened to Me

Much of the personal, social, cultural, professional, and political divisiveness we experience around race would lessen significantly if White people weren't so quick to disbelieve the experiences of people who aren't White.

This happened to me.

No, it didn't.

This happened to me.

There's no way that happened to you.

This happened to me.

It didn't happen to me so it couldn't have happened to you.

This happened to me.

What's your ulterior motive?

This happened to me.

You're trying to game the system.

This happened to me.

That's not a problem anymore.

This happened to me.

I don't understand how that could have happened to you.

This happened to me.

I don't believe you.

The status quo perpetuation machine operating at full capacity.

...continued

White people who almost always have more political power, more social capital, more positional authority, more professional influence, casually and easily dismissing the lived realities and legitimate experiences of people who aren't White.

And then when people who aren't White speak up, they are gaslit, further dismissed, and labeled divisive.

Ad infinitum.

White people new to the racial equity discussion often ask, "What can I do to help?"

Start by believing people who aren't White. Validating someone's truth makes more of a difference than you can imagine.

As If...

"If they would've just complied..."

As if compliance ever guarantees safety. Or survival.

As if the origin of police departments wasn't to protect the property—including slaves—of rich White people.

As if the primary purpose of police departments didn't evolve to keep freed slaves in line once slavery ended.

As if there aren't direct links between police departments and White Supremacist groups like the KKK since 1865 that continues today.

As if White men like Dylann Roof, John Cowell, and Travis McMichael weren't casually—politely—apprehended by police officers after they murdered Black people.

As if people arguing the compliance line of thinking aren't recruiters and hiring managers and VPs and executives and board members in Fortune 500 companies who have the power and influence to create a more equitable world, but choose not to.

As if Black people aren't expected to be "professional" and comply by not wearing dreadlocks or never getting angry or always code-switching.

As if complying to the norms and expectations of a White supremacist society is conducive to the intellectual, emotional, physical, and mental health of those who comply.

As if we live in a meritocracy that treats everyone equally.

As if compliance is the answer to our current racial problems.

Historical Events
Are Current Events

"That happened a long time ago. Why are we still talking about it?"

"We can't change history. Let's move on."

"Things are better now. Stop complaining."

As if the murders of Emmett Till and Medgar Evers and Malcolm X and Martin Luther King Jr. and Fred Hampton and Carole Robertson and Cynthia Wesley and Denise McNair and Addie Mae Collins and...

As if their deaths and why they were killed have no relevance today.

As if they were just sad and unjust historical events—people we've recognized, honored, and eulogized, who are no longer present in our imagination.

As if the so-called current events are somehow disconnected from the so-called historical events.

As if there's a clear delineation between a current event and a historical event.

When does that happen? The minute after? The next day? The next month, year, decade?

They're all current events. It's all happening now. What's happening now happened now and now and now for centuries.

We only say it happened then to absolve ourselves from exploring its significance on what's happening today.

When do the murders of George Floyd and Breonna Taylor and Ahmaud Arbery become historical events?

When we get tired of talking about them?

I feel change coming.

Break the Loop

The reason it's difficult for majority group members to be antiracist is because they don't believe the lived experiences of people from underrepresented groups.

They view everyone's experience through the same lens—their own!

When they hear about someone else's experience, they apply the perspective of their lived experience and realize that the two experiences don't match up. Then they dismiss the other person's lived experience because it doesn't align with their own.

One of the main reasons for this is that people don't consume content and media that provides a wide range of perspectives from people "not like them."

If I'm a White man and I've never read a book by a Black person, listened to a podcast by a Black person, or gone to an event centering Black people, I miss out on the dynamism and nuance and specificity of the Black experience.

I then bring this lack of exposure and lack of understanding to my interactions with Black people in the workplace and I am unable to appreciate and empathize with the experiences that Black people share.

It's an unending spiraling, devolving, and perpetuating loop that always starts and ends in the same place.

A place that centers White experiences, and marginalizes any and all Black experiences.

Break the loop. Educate yourself. Do better.

Listen to Black Women

In Crystal Fleming's book *How To Be Less Stupid About Race,* she has a chapter entitled "Listen to Black Women."

The opening sentence says this:

"White (male) supremacy socializes us to devalue the critical insights of Black women and girls."

So, if I'm a White male, which I am, I have a choice.

I can play my part to take this truth seriously. And I can work to reverse it.

I can stand up to White male hegemony. I can disrupt old boys' networks. I can challenge bro culture.

I can speak out when I witness or hear about Black women and girls not being given credit for their insights and intellectual contributions.

I can proactively and intentionally center the perspectives of Black women and girls. I can challenge my White male colleagues (and anyone else) who regularly dismiss, discourage, and disregard the efforts of Black women and girls.

I can read books and articles written by Black women. I can follow Black women on LinkedIn and Twitter. I can listen to podcasts centering Black women's perspectives.

I can evolve my consciousness and expand my understanding of "normal."

Or, I can shrug off that statement, not reflect on its truth, and continue to not care about the inequitable and oppressive world that I have contributed to.

I know what I'm doing. What about you?

What Should I Do?

"White people want to start with strategy.
White people want the answer, but it has to emerge."

– Resmaa Menakem

What should I do?

You should get intimate with other White people.

But what should I *do*?

You should develop your awareness.

But what should I *do*?

You should self-reflect on how you perpetuate racism.

But what should I *do*?

You should evolve your consciousness.

But what should I *do*?

You should unlearn what you've been taught—or not taught—about what racism actually is, how it manifests, and how it negatively impacts people of all races.

But what should I *do*?

You should examine who you were, who you are, who you're becoming, why you care, what you need to learn, and what's your role in the struggle.

But what should I *do*?

You should challenge your White family members, friends, colleagues, and community members and stay present in uncomfortable conversations.

But what should I *do*?

...continued

You should create a new normal for yourself—intentionally surround yourself with non-White perspectives, books, news, and media.

But what should I *do*?

You should stop asking what you should *do*, and start asking who you should *be*.

But I know who I am.

You should dismantle who you *think* you are.

But that might take a long time.

Exactly.

Don't Just Do Something, Sit There

"Don't just do something, sit there." – Sylvia Boorstein

Is action bias a dominant feature in your social justice and antiracism work?

The bias that leads you to "do something" because you're supposed to "do something."

The bias that leads you to believe that because you did something—one thing, or maybe two things—that the work is over.

The bias that leads you to believe that someone can or should or will give you a concrete list of "do's" and "don'ts" that you can laminate and hang by your desk as a guide to continue doing something.

The bias that leads you to dismiss ongoing intentional and selective reading and listening and media consumption and self-educating and immersing and learning and evolving and self-assessing as "not doing anything" or "not doing enough."

The bias that leads you to conflate performative allyship that is visible and commentable and likable with the true, deep, consistent self-development work that isn't as visible and laudable and commendable.

The bias that leads to boxes being checked and status quos "status quoing."

The bias that provides you with allyship cookies and pins.

The bias that mocks self-reflection and meditation and self-actualization and committing to who you truly want to be.

The bias that perpetuates racial inequity and injustice.

Walking the Talk

I've been a fan of Brené Brown for several years. Her work on empathy, vulnerability, courage, and shame has influenced my work.

And lately, I've been impressed with her antiracism and social justice work.

As much as I admire her work, I always felt she could go deeper with a social justice and racial equity lens. But she rarely did.

Until now.

And, she's embraced it. She has fluency. She's not just talking out of her ass or flaunting her celebrity or being a performative ally.

When she talks with her podcast guests about this stuff, she totally gets it. She understands her role as a White woman in this space.

She listens, she amplifies, she shows empathy and compassion. She validates the lived experiences of people who have been marginalized and oppressed.

And it all feels genuine, sincere, relevant. She walks her talk.

Hearing her speak so fluently about the issues makes me wonder how many other everyday White people have not been stepping up.

People who may not have Brené's platform, but who have power and privilege to be allies, accomplices, co-conspirators.

People who stay silent and perpetuate the status quo. Who don't use their voice to affect change. Who don't challenge the dominant narrative. Who are okay with the norm.

That wouldn't be you, would it?

You Are Amy Cooper Too

You are Amy Cooper too.

You are Amy Cooper when you don't consider the Black candidate for the role.

You are Amy Cooper when you clutch your purse walking past a Black man on the street.

You are Amy Cooper when you talk over your Black colleague at the team meeting.

You are Amy Cooper when you go to the ninety-eight percent White golf/swim/tennis club with all your White friends.

You are Amy Cooper when you promote your less talented, less experienced White colleague instead of your Black colleague.

You are Amy Cooper when you don't consider letting your kids play with the Black kids outside of school.

You are Amy Cooper when you try to tone police the concerns of your Black colleagues' experiences of microaggressions.

You are Amy Cooper when the last fifty books you've read have been by White people.

You are Amy Cooper when you gossip about your Black colleague to your shared supervisor to get the promotion ahead of her.

You are Amy Cooper when you say you "don't see color."

You are Amy Cooper when you say, "it's a meritocracy."

You are Amy Cooper when you don't self-reflect on the advantages you've gained because of your unearned privilege and power.

You will continue to be Amy Cooper until you do your personal development work to not be Amy Cooper anymore.

Unapologetically White

Some White people have a hard time understanding why a Black person would declare that they are unapologetically Black.

While I would never speak for any individual Black person, or Black people as a group, I suspect it stems from having to navigate an unapologetically White world that ceaselessly marginalizes, others, oppresses, denies, murders, fetishizes, and appropriates blackness.

Unapologetically White legislators who pass and uphold anti-Black laws and policies.

Unapologetically White politicians who make anti-Black speeches and incite anti-Black activities.

Unapologetically White boards who deadbolt their anti-Black old boys' network doors.

Unapologetically White executives who sit at anti-Black tables and make anti-Black decisions.

Unapologetically White cops who kneel on the neck of Black people until they die.

Unapologetically White vigilantes who murder Black joggers.

Unapologetically White dog walkers who weaponize their anti-Black privilege.

And the list goes on.

Of course, this unapologetic whiteness and unapologetic anti-blackness is rarely said out loud.

It's implied, condoned, expected—baked into the fabric of our existence.

It doesn't need to be spoken. It just is.

And is and is and is and is...

Until White people decide it no longer is.

All Lives Matter

All lives matter.

Unless you're a Black man checking on your kids in your car in Kenosha, Wisconsin. Then that life gets seven bullets in the back at point-blank range.

All lives matter.

Unless you're a Black man jogging down a road in Brunswick, Georgia. Then that life gets two shotgun blasts to the stomach from vigilantes who say you're a robber.

All lives matter.

Unless you're a Black man who fell asleep in your car at the Wendy's drive through in Atlanta. Then that life gets chased down and shot in the back while running away.

All lives matter.

Unless you're a Black woman sleeping in your apartment in Louisville. Then that life ends in a barrage of police gunfire after they batter down your door.

All lives matter.

Unless you're a Black man arrested for allegedly using a counterfeit bill in Minneapolis. Then that life gets kneeled on until there's no air left to breathe.

All lives matter.

Unless it's a life that an individual or a group of individuals or a police department or a judicial system or a legal system or a political system or a governmental institution or an administration or history says doesn't matter.

Then, I guess, it seems that not all lives matter.

Which is why we say Black lives matter.

Some folks need to hear that message over and over again.

Dear White People

Dear White people,

I get it. You don't like to talk about racism. It makes you feel uncomfortable. You wish it would just go away—the racism, sure, but mostly the talking about it.

You think the talking about racism is why there's still racism.

Which is totally fucking stupid and illogical—not to mention disrespectful and dismissive and harmful.

But, hey, it's easier to say things like:

"Slavery happened a long time ago," and "We had a Black president," and "It's a meritocracy," and "I believe in personal responsibility," and all kinds of other ignorant stuff...

...than it is to actually believe the experiences of people who are harmed by racism every day.

You avoid conversations that talk about your privilege and power and social capital because, hey, you've worked hard, or you grew up poor, or you've been rejected, or look at Oprah, or—"Mommy, they're bullying me!"

If you examined your beliefs a fraction as often as you expressed them, you'd discover you don't actually believe them.

But you're not that self-aware. You don't read. You're not curious. Empathy? Not so much.

You know why I know all this about you? Because I'm White, and I used to believe all this stupid shit too.

Until I got over myself, woke the fuck up, and changed.

So when are you gonna do the same?

He Was a Black Man
Running Down Our Road

Emergency call operator: "Was Ahmaud Arbery committing a crime?"

Travis and Gregory McMichael: "He's a Black man running down our road."

Was Trayvon Martin committing a crime?

He was a Black teenager wearing a hoodie.

Was Tamir Rice committing a crime?

He was a twelve-year-old Black boy with a toy gun.

Was Sandra Bland committing a crime?

She was a Black woman who failed to signal a lane change.

Was Eric Garner committing a crime?

He was a Black man "suspected" of selling single cigarettes without tax stamps.

Was Michael Brown committing a crime?

He was a Black man walking down the middle of the street.

Was Oscar Grant committing a crime?

He was a Black man on BART enjoying a New Year's Eve celebration.

Was Stephon Clark committing a crime?

He was a Black man talking on a cell phone at his grandma's house.

Was Philando Castile committing a crime?

He was a Black man telling a police officer he had a firearm but wasn't reaching for it.

...continued

Why are so many White people afraid of Black people?

Because they don't see them as human.

Why are Black people afraid of White people's fear?

Because it leads to being killed.

When is it going to stop?

When White people see the humanity in Black people.

Section 10: An Invitation to Reflect

1. When is calling people out on their racism a better option than calling people in?

2. Why is it so often uncomfortable to call people out on their racism? What are the risks? What are the benefits?

3. Have you ever been called out for doing or saying something racist? How did you respond? What did you learn from the experience?

4. Who do you want to be in the antiracism struggle? How are you continually working towards becoming that person?

5. Are you willing to see the humanity in all people? Why or why not?

Afterward: An Invitation to Act

Okay, what do you do now? If you've read this far, I trust that you have an emerging clarity about what you can do to confront racism. You've read my stories, learned about my past, cringed at my mistakes, learned of my lessons, and joined me on my journey. You've gotten an insider view into my experiences and my psyche and my worldview and my life. You've witnessed how I've been shaped and molded and influenced, and by whom and by what. I have exposed you to my approach and my values and my principles, and you have observed what's worked for me and what hasn't. You've seen how I have evolved my consciousness, how I have navigated change and uncertainty, how I found my conviction, how I discovered my voice, how I understand and embody and articulate my authentic antiracist narrative. You have clarity about why confronting racism is important to me, why I'm immovable in my commitment to seeing the humanity in every single person.

But, this book is about you. It's about you getting clarity about why confronting racism is important to you. It's about you articulating why you are immovable in your commitment to seeing the humanity in every person. It's about you evolving your consciousness, finding your conviction, discovering your voice, and understanding and embodying your authentic antiracist narrative.

I can't tell you how to do that, and neither can anybody else. It has to come from you. It has to come from your lived experiences and your observations and your mistakes and your lessons. Decide why and how you're going to confront racism, and be committed to embarking on a lifelong antiracist journey.

Come to your understanding and appreciation that at its core antiracism work is social justice work, that racism persists not because of racist individuals who are mean and ignorant and malicious, but because of racist systems that White individuals intentionality built on the premise of White supremacy. These systems have normalized whiteness and racism in all its forms. These systems perpetuate the status quo. These systems have been operating as intended for hundreds of years to oppress, marginalize, subjugate, and divide.

Understand that the people in power are not incentivized to relinquish their power and privilege and social capital, are not genuinely interested in equity and justice, do not believe in leveling the playing field, are not going to cooperate in any efforts that are working toward dismantling the systems that perpetuate their power and privilege and social capital. Understand that these realities necessitate that your antiracism and social justice work be more urgent, more accelerated, more elevated. This means being more urgent in accelerating and elevating your cultural fluency by reading and listening and watching and immersing and being in alignment with people from marginalized communities.

Commit to being an advocate, an accomplice, a co-conspirator, to being in true solidarity with all people and communities on the downside of power. Commit to understanding the issues on an individual and systemic level, not just intellectually but interpersonally, so that you get to a place where you see yourself not as a savior or a philanthropist, but as someone whose personal liberation is wrapped up in the liberation of all people who are not free from the grips of White supremacy.

To be able to do all that requires emotional intelligence. Confronting racism requires intense and consistent listening to and hearing and believing the lived experiences and stories of people "not like you." It requires empathy, compassion and holding space for people to share their truths. It requires non-judgment and curiosity and building trust and connection. It requires cultivating genuine relationships, communicating with intentionality and humility, not centering ourselves, amplifying underrepresented voices and stories and experiences.

Confronting racism requires that we continually reassess, re-evaluate, and re-examine our motives and actions and habits and patterns of behavior to recognize when and how and where we are contributing to an antiracist world and when and how and where we are perpetuating systems of White supremacy. Confronting racism requires that we are constantly evolving our consciousness and are always self-aware of who we are, how others perceive us, and who we are becoming.

Confronting racism also requires that we get comfortable being uncomfortable, that we are able to sit with uncertainty, that we don't fall back on our privilege and check out of important conversations. Confronting racism requires that we stay present and focused, that we are constantly aware of our emotions and triggers and feelings. It requires that we be mindful of how we show up in the world and how and if our intentions align with our impact. It requires that we not conflate dialogue with debate, that we not confuse passion with purpose, that we do not let our anger and righteousness, brought about by the injustices and inequities that we see all around us, lead us down a devolving path of cognitive squalor. Confronting racism requires that we don't get distracted by trivial arguments and interactions that divert us from the meaningful work that is needed.

Confronting racism requires that we cultivate equanimity to show up with purpose and be influential with the people and within the communities and systems in our spheres of impact.

And perhaps most importantly, confronting racism demands that we know our antiracist narrative, know who we are, understand why we care about confronting racism, and articulate why we're doing any of this in the first place.

Confronting racism demands that we develop our antiracism story so that we can know our antiracism story so that we can share our antiracism story so that the power and authenticity of our antiracism story can change the world. Discovering and owning and telling our antiracism story demands ongoing self-reflection, deep vulnerability, a commitment to immovable values and principles, and unabashed devotion to embodying our compelling truth. Because if we don't know our truth, and if we can't share our truth with others, and if we can't live our truth with confidence and conviction, why should we expect anyone else to believe us, to connect with us, to trust us, to take us seriously? The answer is we can't and we shouldn't.

There are plenty of bloviating performative allies out there spewing all kinds of inconsequential platitudes, crafting all kinds of boilerplate statements of meaninglessness, tearfully choking out all kinds of trite irrelevancies. People who haven't bothered to reflect on who they are and why they care, who haven't done their self-development work, and who are in the end contributing nothing but intrusive noise to the antiracism struggle.

But that's not you. You're different than that. You're better than that. You're more committed than that. You've read this book. And you've read, or will read, many other books. You've listened. You've heard. You've believed people's stories. You've immersed yourself in communities of people not like you. You've reflected. You've discussed ideas and concepts and frameworks and solutions with others. You've come to understand why racism exists. You've come to understand how you're going to confront racism. You're ready to see the humanity in every single person. You've explored what motivates you, what inspires you, what galvanizes you. You've decided to change who you are. You've evolved your consciousness. You're different now. You think differently. You feel differently. You're ready to act differently.

And the world is waiting for you to act. So get to it.

About the Author

Jared Karol is the founder of JaredKarol.com, a consulting firm specializing in guiding White people to confront racism and be unapologetic antiracists. As a trusted advisor, he guides executives, people managers, and dedicated change agents at Fortune 500 companies, startups, and nonprofits. A sought-after professional speaker, panel moderator, leadership coach, and facilitator of difficult conversations, Jared's storytelling approach inspires and influences individuals and groups worldwide. An avid reader, accomplished musician, and active meditator, he lives with his family in the San Francisco Bay Area. Learn how you can bring Jared to your organization at JaredKarol.com.

Acknowledgements

My name is on the cover of this book, but I could not have written it without the guidance and support of many people.

The original title of this book was "A White Guy Talking About Race and Other Stuff That Matters." Naomi Raquel Enright, you asked me, "Aren't you really talking about rac*ism*, not race?" Of course I was! That shifted immensely how I thought of what this book could become. Not long after that, Steve Mudd, you asked me, "Are you just talking about racism, or are you confronting racism?" Damn right, I'm confronting it. "Confronting Racism" not only became part of the title, but shaped the entire structure and flow of the book. Kayla Lee, the subtitle of this book came from a LinkedIn message you sent me at the beginning of 2021: "What you share is an invitation for reflection and/or action." Which is exactly what I always intend to do. Naomi, Steve, and Kayla, I am very grateful for these contributions that have helped shape my thinking on how I went about writing this book.

Dr. Nika White, way back in May of 2020, you were the first person to suggest that I turn my writings into a book, planting the seed.

Rajkumari Neogy, you practically demanded that I write this book. Thank you for your consistent and loving pressure for me to contribute my insights to the world. And, thank you for letting me borrow (steal) STFU (Seek to Fully Understand) from you—a humorous way to make a very serious point.

Dianne Tennen, Dr. Jen Howard, Erica Karol, and Dr. Nika White, thank you for reading the entire early draft of this book. Your feedback, comments, and suggestions helped improve this book immensely. With your insights, I moved things around, cut stuff that didn't work, added reflection questions at the end of each section, and paid more attention to my tone throughout.

Autymn Harris, Emily Weltman, Kayla Lee, and Kirk Lorie, your input on specific sections of the early draft was helpful as well. I appreciate you taking the time to provide feedback.

Richard Tardif, your expert editing lifted this book immeasurably. You helped me tighten my language, be more consistent in my tone, and eliminate tautologies and other redundancies, while honoring my authentic writing style and voice. I know this book would be in a much worse state without your expertise. I miss our Friday morning editing sessions.

Carolyn Flower, I am grateful to you and Oxygen Publishing for guiding me through the entire publishing process. From our very first call to seeing the completed book on the shelves, you believed in me and this book. I appreciate your thought partnership, stewardship, and publishing industry mastery.

Wendy Horng Brawer, our conversations helped shape my views on the dual journeys of cultural fluency and personal development. I'm grateful for our collaborations.

Jonathan Mahan, Keishla Ceaser-Jones, and Kehsi Iman Wilson, our conversations on racism and vulnerability both supported and informed my views in this book. And Kehsi Iman, I'm sure you can see how our collaboration on the interconnectedness of mindfulness and social justice shows up throughout the book. I'm grateful to you all.

Michael Margolis, it is because of you and your work that I center storytelling in my antiracism work. I learned from you that storytelling isn't just a "nice to have" but an essential element in building connection and trust, sustaining relationships, and breaking down barriers so we can create inclusive communities where everyone can thrive.

Kay Fabella, when you first shared with me the idea that some people are still in the "bomb-throwing stage of the revolution," you immediately gave me language to shape how I talked about my evolution in doing this work. You no doubt can see your influence throughout this book.

Elliot Zanger, I remember the days when instead of doing our editorial work we would take online geography quizzes and have pseudo-philosophical discussions about how we should be paid a better salary. You said that if we valued making more money, we would get another job. But we didn't, so making more money was just an ideal. That stuck with me, as you can see in the first vignette in Section Six. I've applied that lens of values vs. ideals to everything I do—to hold myself accountable and to make better decisions. I appreciate our friendship.

Many other friends, colleagues, thought partners, and collaborators have contributed in some way to this book becoming a reality. Aaron Clark, Amanda Townsend, Cass Averill, Cindy Owyoung, Corey Ponder, Dominique Hollins, Joel Brown, Mariama Beemer, Mercedes Adams, Rachel Kjack, Sumayyah Emeh-Edu, Susan Cooney, and Tet Salva, I see your humanity and I appreciate our relationships. May we continue our collaborations indefinitely.

I've been fortunate to have wonderful mentors and coaches who have supported, inspired, and challenged me to contribute optimally to the world. Karen Colaric, you helped cement and expand my understanding of social justice principles when I was teaching sixth grade humanities. Julie Gleeson, you challenged me to become an entrepreneur, pushed me to believe in abundance instead of scarcity, and helped me appreciate that all meaningful work begins from the inside. Kyle Elliott, you encouraged me to be strong in my principles and values, to be either a "hell yes" or a "hell no" because no one cares about about a "hell maybe." Thank you all for your insights and your confidence in me.

Karen Van Dyne, you probably don't remember me, the twenty-something who accompanied his dad to the gay men's meditation circles on Sanchez Street at the end of the last century. But I remember your kindness, soft presence, and equanimity. You unknowingly started me on a mindfulness journey that continues to this day. I am forever grateful for that.

Eric Delore and Dolores Zacchoni, as two of my dad's best friends, I learned what it means to love and support someone unconditionally, no matter what they're going through, including dying. I will be forever grateful to you, and I love you both.

Amy Perl, on a warm summer night in the mountains outside of Boulder, Colorado in 1993, you changed the directory of my life forever. Your response of "big fucking deal" to the news that my dad was gay allowed me to start seeing the humanity in every single person. I love you and will always be grateful for our friendship.

Dad, I think you'd be proud of who I've become. Thank you for pushing me and challenging me to see that there is indeed more to life than El Cajon. I love you and miss you, and I'm doing my best to carry on your legacy.

Erica, Juliet, and Max, you are my everything. Thank you for your support and unconditional love. I wrote this book for you. I love you all very much.

References

Achebe, Chinua. (1958) Things Fall Apart. McDowell, Obelensky.

Adichie, Chimamanda Ngozi. (2009) The Danger of a Single Story. TEDGlobal.

Adichie, Chimamanda Ngozi. (2018) Dear Ijeawele, or A Feminist Manifesto in Fifteen Suggestions. Anchor.

Anderson, Carol. (2016) White Rage: The Unspoken Truth of Our Racial Divide. Bloomsbury Publishing.

Baldwin, James. (1963) The Fire Next Time. The Dial Press.

Boorstein, Sylvia. (1996) Don't Just Do Something, Sit There: A Mindfulness Retreat. Harper One.

Box, Heather and Mocine-McQueen, Julian. (2017) The Million Person Project. http://www.millionpersonproject.org/.

Brown, Brené. (2019) The Call to Courage. Netflix.

Brown, Brené. (2012) Daring Greatly: How the Courage to Be Vulnerable Transforms the Way We Live, Love, Parent, and Lead. Penguin Putnam Inc.

Brown, Brené. (2020) Interview with Laverne Cox. Unlocking Us podcast.

Brown, Brené and Burke, Tarana (eds). (2021) You Are Your Best Thing: Vulnerability, Shame Resilience, and the Black Experience. Random House.

Brown, Jennifer. (2019) How to Be an Inclusive Leader: Your Role in Creating Cultures of Belonging Where Everyone Can Thrive. Berrett-Koehler Publishers, Inc.

Chödrön, Pema. (2002) Comfortable With Uncertainty: 108 Teachings on Cultivating Fearlessness and Compassion. Penguin Random House LLC.

Chödrön, Pema. (2012) Living Beautifully with Uncertainty and Change. Penguin Random House LLC

Confucius. (1998) The Analects. Penguin Classics.

Cooper, Brittney. (2018) Eloquent Rage: A Black Femenist Discovers Her Superpower. St. Martin's Press.

DiAngelo, Robin. (2020) Is This the Moment?: A Conversation with Resmaa Menakem and Robin DiAngelo. Education for Racial Equity.

DiAngelo, Robin. (2018) White Fragility: Why It's So Hard for White People to Talk About Racism. Beacon Press.

Eddo-Lodge, Reni. (2019) Why I'm No Longer Talking to White People About Race. Bloomsbury Publishing.

Ellison, Ralph. (1952) Invisible Man. Random House.

Fails, Jimmie. (2019) The Last Black Man in San Francisco. A24 and Plan B Entertainment.

Fearon, Clinton. (2006) Sleeping Lion. Vision. Kool Yu Foot.

Fitzgerald, F. Scott. (1945) The Crack-Up. New Directions.

Fleming, Crystal. (2018) How to Be Less Stupid About Race. Beacon Press.

Frankl, Viktor. (1959) Man's Search for Meaning. Beacon Press.

Gandhi, Mahatma. (1982) Gandhi. Columbia Pictures.

Grant, Adam. (2020) Authenticity is a Double-Edged Sword. WorkLife with Adam Grant.

hooks, bell. (1994) Sisters of the Yam: Black Women and Self-Recovery. South End Press.

Hoskin, Maia Niguel, Ph.D. (2020) Performative Activism is the New 'Color-Blind' Band-Aid for White Fragility. Medium.

Ivins, Molly. (2015) What is the Aim of Satire? Alexandra Petri in the Washington Post.

Keats, John. (1817) Letter to brothers George and Thomas.

Kendi, Ibram. (2020) A Battle Between the Two Souls of America. The Atlantic.

Kendi, Ibram. (2019) How to Be An Antiracist. One World.

Kendi, Ibram. (2016) Stamped From the Beginning: The Definitive History of Racist Ideas in America. Nation Books.

Kjack, Rachel. (2021) Conversation with the author in March 2021.

Lorde, Audre. (1982) Learning from the 60s. Speech at Harvard University.

Lorde, Audre. (2013) Sister Outsider: Essays and Speeches. Ten Speed Press.

Lythcott-Haims, Julie. (2018) Real American: A Memoir. St. Martin's Griffin.

Magee, Rhonda. (2019) The Inner Work of Racial Justice: Healing Ourselves and Transforming Our Communities Through Mindfulness. Tarcher Perigee.

Mali, Taylor. (2003) Totally Like Whatever. Conviction. Words Worth Ink & The Wordsmith Press.

Margolis, Michael. (2019) Story 10X: Turn the Impossible Into the Inevitable. Storied.

Marley, Bob. (1976) War. Rastaman Vibration. Island Records.

Menakem, Resmaa. (2020) Is This the Moment?: A Conversation with Resmaa Menakem and Robin DiAngelo. Education for Racial Equity.

Menakem, Resmaa. (2020) Notice the Rage; Notice the Silence. On Being with Krista Tippett podcast.

Miguel Ruiz Jr., Don. (2013) The Five Levels of Attachment: Toltec Wisdom for the Modern World. Hierophant Publishing.

Oluo, Ijeoma. (2019) So You Want to Talk About Race. Seal Press.

Painter, Nell Irvin. (2010) The History of White People. W. W. Norton & Company Inc.

Plato. (2018) The Apology of Socrates. Forgotten Books.

Plett, Heather. (2020) The Art of Holding Space: A Practice of Love, Liberations, and Leadership. Page Two.

Rivera, Gabby. (2020) Brené Brown interview. Unlocking Us podcast.

Rivera, Gabby. (2016) Juliet Takes a Breath. Riverdale Avenue Books.

Rock, Chris. (2016) Opening monologue. 88th Academy Awards.

Suzuki, Shunryu. (1970) Zen Mind, Beginner's Mind. Shambhala Publications Inc.

Tatum, Beverley, Dr. (1997) Why Are All the Black Kids Sitting Together in the Cafeteria? Basic Books.

Unknown. "You've changed! I'd hope so!" artwork.

Walker, Brian Browne. (1992) Hua Hu Ching: The Unknown Teachings of Lao Tzu. Harper San Francisco.

Wallace, Michelle. (1978) Black Macho and The Myth of the SuperWoman. Dial Press.

Yunus, Muhammad. (1998) Banker to the Poor: Micro-Lending and the Battle Against World Poverty. Autumn Press.

CPSIA information can be obtained
at www.ICGtesting.com
Printed in the USA
BVHW042302291121
622764BV00013B/605